Healing Made Simple

Michael Cameneti

insight
PUBLISHING GROUP

Tulsa, Oklahoma

HEALING MADE SIMPLE

Healing Made Simple by Michael Cameneti
Published by Insight Publishing Group
8801 S. Yale, Suite 410
Tulsa, OK 74137
918-493-1718

Unless otherwise indicated, all Scripture quotations in
this volume are from the *King James Version* of the Bible.

Scripture taken from *THE AMPLIFIED BIBLE, Old Testament*
copyright © 1965, 1987 by the Zondervan Corporation. The
Amplified *New Testament* copyright © 1958, 1987 by The
Lockman Foundation. Used by permission. Scripture quotations marked NKJV are from the New King James Version of
the Bible. Copyright © 1979, 1980, 1982 by Thomas Nelson
Inc., publishers. Used by permission.

ISBN 1-930027-97-4
Library of Congress catalog card number: 2003102791

Printed in the United States of America

DEDICATION

I would like to dedicate this book to the members of Canton Christian Fellowship. Thank you for being such wonderful sheep, you make the job of a pastor a complete pleasure.

CONTENTS

FOREWORD

Having known Michael Cameneti before he came to Jesus and knowing him now after, we can say his life has completely changed. Before Jesus, Mike lived totally for the devil. Now, he lives his life totally for Jesus.

Mike loves to diligently study the Word of God, but even better—he lives it. On the subjects of faith and healing he has not only head knowledge, but a working knowledge that has produced results in his life as well as in the lives of others.

You are going to like this book! The practical insights that he shares will help and inspire you as they did us.

Tony and Patsy Cameneti

PREFACE

As a pastor of a local church, it has always been my desire to take the subject of Healing and make it as simple as possible. As you read this book, it is my prayer that the simple truths taught throughout the chapters, will help you to receive your healing from God.

My wife and I have experienced God's healing power in our own lives, and have watched the healing power touch our children's lives. We have also seen the power of God touch countless lives within our church. When our son was born we were told he would most likely die from a condition he had been born with. That was over 21 years ago. Today, every time we look back to when we were given the report and then look at him now as a young adult, we're reminded of what an awesome God we serve!

God is a good God and He wants to do the same for any who will believe Him. May God bless you as you read this book.

Pastor Michael Cameneti

CHAPTER ONE

WHERE DOES SICKNESS COME FROM?

When I was in high school, I studied geometry. I memorized axioms and learned how to prove geometric theorems. But after I finished high school, I paid no attention to geometry, and it slipped away. Today, I don't know anything about it, even though I was familiar with it at one time.

The same thing can happen to a spiritual truth. I can receive a lot of good teaching and become very familiar with an area of the Word, but if I stop paying attention to it, it can drift away.

Hebrews 2:1 says, *"Therefore we ought to give the more earnest heed to the things which we have heard, lest at any time we should let them slip."*

The verse tells us to pay close attention to the spiritual truths we have learned and make an effort to hold on to them. Otherwise, they will escape. Like flowing water, they will slip away.

The Lord has stirred me to offer you some key truths regarding what we need to know about healing *to be healed*, and I am excited about it. But I can almost hear you thinking, *I've already heard about healing. I already know about that.*

However, healing is an area of the Bible where truth can slip away. In His teaching ministry, Jesus returned frequently to the subject of healing, and I believe we need to return to it too. Otherwise, we can become careless about it and allow it to leave our lives.

Destroyed for Lack of Knowledge

Hosea 4:6 says, *"My people are destroyed for lack of knowledge: because thou hast rejected knowledge, I will also reject thee."*

We have a wonderful covenant with God, and under the terms of this covenant, God will never reject us, no matter how indifferent to His Word we become. However, we will lose the benefits of the covenant if we reject the covenant's promises.

For example, the Bible teaches that God wants us to prosper. Scripture says that He wants to pour out blessings upon us and give us the desires of our hearts. However, we as children of God can say, "I believe that financial prosperity is carnal. I reject the prosperity message." We will still be God's children and will go to Heaven when we die, but we have rejected the knowledge of prosperity and will never prosper.

Likewise, we can reject the knowledge of healing. We can say, "I believe God uses sickness as a way of teaching and perfecting me. I have to accept the sickness He brings. It is my cross to bear." We will still be God's children, and He will still love us, but we have rejected the knowedge of healing and will not be healed.

Lack of knowledge destroys people. If we don't receive knowledge, we won't collect its benefits. That's the foundational truth of Hosea 4:6.

However, we gain additional understanding about Hosea 4:6 when we study the Hebrew word for "destroyed." The Hebrew word doesn't mean *to demolish* or *to annihilate*, as we might expect. It means *to silence.*

Any time we have a lack of knowledge about a subject, we have a tendency to avoid talking about it. For example, if I don't know anything about baseball, I won't want to talk about it, even if I am with someone who is an authority on baseball. In fact, when I am with this person, I will probably hope that the subject of baseball doesn't come up. However, if I am a baseball fan and know about the sport, I will be eager to have a conversation with someone who is an authority.

Of course, knowledge of baseball does not have eternal consequences, but spiritual knowledge does.

Our covenant with God is all about confession. Proclaiming the truth is a big part of acting on faith.

Romans 10:9 and 10 says, *"If thou shalt confess with thy mouth the Lord Jesus, and shalt believe in thine heart that God hath raised Him from the dead, thou shalt be saved. For with the heart man believeth unto righteousness, and with the mouth, confession is made unto salvation."*

Mark 11:23 says that we can speak to a mountain of impossibility and watch the mountain fall into the sea.

When we embrace spiritual truth, we have a tendency to talk about it, and our faith-filled words produce powerful results.

However, when we reject knowledge, our rejection produces spiritual silence, or spiritual muteness, and this silence neutralizes us.

The Origin of Sickness

If I asked you, "Where does sickness come from?" you would probably reply, "Sickness comes from the devil," and you would be correct. The Bible clearly teaches that Satan is the author of sickness.

The Bible talks about a demonic spirit of infirmity that binds people with sickness and disease. Jesus came to release us from the spirit of infirmity.

When God created us, He made us in His own image, and He made us good. Genesis 1:31 says that when God looked at everything He had made, He approved of it *completely*. Everything in His creation, including man, was perfectly suitable.

God did not create illness, and He did not want people to get sick and die. He wanted man to live forever on earth. However, God gave dominion over the earth to Adam, and Adam disobeyed God. We often refer to this event as "the great fall of mankind" because it brought the curse of sickness and death into the world.

"And Dying, You Shall Die"

Genesis 2:9 says, *"Out of the ground made the Lord God to grow every tree that is pleasant to the sight and good for food; the tree of life also in the midst of the garden, and the tree of knowledge of good and evil."*

God placed Adam in the Garden of Eden to dress and keep it. He commanded, *"Of every tree of the garden thou mayest freely eat, but of the tree of the knowledge of good and evil thou shalt not eat of it; for in the day that thou eatest thereof, THOU SHALT SURELY DIE"* (Gen. 2:16,17).

In the Hebrew, this passage is best translated, "And dying, you shall die." It refers to two deaths.

God was warning Adam that if he ate from the tree of the knowledge of good and evil, he would die spiritually, and the spiritual death would cause him to die physically.

Then in Genesis 3, Satan appeared in the Garden, and his message was the opposite of what God had said. Satan said to the woman, Eve, "You shall *not* surely die."

The devil always tells us the opposite of what God says. He always says, "You're strong enough. You're clever enough. If you do it, you'll be okay. No matter what God says, you shall *not* surely die."

This is his strategy.

In Genesis 3:1, Satan is called a "serpent," and in the Hebrew language, this word means, *the one who deals with thoughts in the mind* or *the one who puts thoughts into the mind.*

When I was a little boy, I thought that Satan took on the form of a snake, slithered up to Eve in the Garden, and started talking to her. But that's not what really happened. Satan worked in Eve's life by placing his thoughts in her mind. He kept saying to her, "What beautiful fruit this is, delicious fruit, desirable fruit. You know you want this fruit. Why should you deny yourself? It will be okay. You can eat from this tree, and it won't harm anything." He tempted her by working on her mind.

If Adam had been the husband and man he should have been, and if Eve had submitted herself to him as his wife, she would have gone to Adam and said, "I'm getting thoughts, Adam. I am beginning to desire the forbidden fruit."

And Adam would have said, "No, Eve. Don't do it."

Instead, Eve ate the fruit and then went to Adam, offering some of it to him. And he didn't resist it. He listened to Eve and just ate the fruit. He didn't do anything to try and stop it.

Often, we are like Adam and Eve. A thought comes, and we don't resist it. Even though it comes from Satan, we passively take it in.

Loosed from Infirmity

Sometimes, we allow things into our lives that we shouldn't allow, and we deal with sicknesses and injuries that are the result of our own poor choices and unwise behavior.

However, we sometimes deal with sicknesses and injuries that are caused by the devil, and these problems, or bondages, are called infirmities.

In Luke 13, for example, Jesus is teaching on the Sabbath in one of the synagogues, and He meets a woman who has had an infirmity for eighteen years. Luke 13:11 says that she was, "...*bowed together, and could in no wise lift up herself.*" She was bent completely forward and could not straighten her body or even look up. She was a "daughter of Abraham," so she had the covenant right to be healthy and blessed. But instead of being strong and vigorous, she was helpless and weak. Like so many people in churches today, she had heard about her covenant rights, but was still sick. Her problem was caused by the devil. The Bible says that a demonic spirit of infirmity had bound her. The devil had tied her up with this infirmity.

When Jesus saw her, He called her to Himself and said, "...Woman, thou art loosed from thine infirmity" (Luke 13:12). Jesus simply said, "That's it. It's done. You're loosed." He laid His hands on her, and, instantly, she was made straight. She realized that God had moved, and she began to rejoice.

I can imagine the hope and the power that began to stir in that place. However, the leader of the synagogue, operating out of a religious spirit, became indignant that Jesus had healed someone on the Sabbath and said to the people, "...There are six days in which men ought to work: in them therefore come and be healed, and not on the sabbath day" (v. 14).

Religion tries to control and restrict the move of God. Religion, which is morally evil, labors to keep you bound.

Jesus responded to the religious leader by calling him a "play actor," or a hypocrite.

The Story of the Good Samaritan

In Luke 10, Jesus uses the story of the Good Samaritan to show the difference between religious behavior, which is bad, and a Spirit-led life, which is good.

In this account, the good Samaritan represents *Jesus*. The oil that He applies to the wounds of the injured man is a type of *salvation*; the wine is a type of *the baptism in the Holy Ghost*; the inn represents *the Church*; and the money that the Samaritan gives the innkeeper is symbolic of *the price Jesus paid when He went to Calvary.* However, before Jesus arrives, religion walks by.

Luke 10:30 talks about a man who went from Jerusalem to Jericho. He fell among thieves, who stripped him of his clothes and belongings, beat him, and went their way, unconcerned that they had left him half dead.

A priest came by, self-righteous and beautifully attired. When he saw the injured man, he crossed over to the other side of the road and hurried on his way.

A well educated, legalistic, puffed up, and self-satisfied Levite came by. He also saw the wounded man, but crossed over to the other side of the road and hurried away.

Two times, religion did nothing to help the man. Two times, religion walked away.

Then the Good Samaritan came by, had *pity and compassion* on the dying traveler, and went to him. He poured oil and wine on the injured man's wounds, dressed them, and then set the man on His own colt and took him to an inn.

He took care of the man, and when it was time for Him to leave, He gave two days' wages to the innkeeper and said, "Take care of him, and whatever more you spend, I myself will repay you when I return."

The Parable of the Good Samaritan is an illustration of what Jesus did for us when He died on the Cross. He put the oil and wine of the Holy Spirit on our wounds. He put us on His own colt and took us to the Church. He paid for two days' (two thousand years) of care and ministry and then said to the Church, "If there's anything more that has to be done, do it and put it on to my charge. When I return (at the end of the Age), I will pay for it all."

Everything was charged to Jesus and put on the Cross. In His mercy, He paid for everything.

If you have mental problems, Jesus has made it possible for you to have deliverance and victory. If you have bone deformities or missing limbs, Jesus has paid for your restoration and recovery. If Satan has robbed you of sight, hearing, or the ability to walk or talk, Jesus wants to give these things back to you. If you are tired or discouraged, Jesus wants to restore your energy and optimism. Jesus wants to give back your strength and good health. He wants to restore everything.

When sickness or disease tries to attack us with symptoms or a bad report, the first thought is usually this: *Why is God doing this?* If we have been taught enough of the Word to know that God didn't give us the sickness, we are tempted to ask, *Why did God release Satan to do this to me?*

These thoughts and frustrations indicate that we still are not settled in our hearts regarding the truth of the Word. God does not cause sickness. Chronic illnesses, chronic fatigue, depression, cancer, heart disease—God is not the author of these things.

James 1:13 says, *"Let no man say when he is tempted, I am tempted OF God; for God cannot be tempted with evil, neither tempteth He any man."*

We gain an understanding of this Bible verse when we study the Greek word for "of." In the Greek, many different words can be translated "of," but the word that is used in this passage is the word "opo," which essentially means, *done in a roundabout or behind-the-scenes way.* In other words, James is saying, "When we are tempted, God is not bringing the temptation, either in a direct or a roundabout way."

Temptation comes from being baited and enticed by Satan. Temptation does not come from God. John 10:10 says that Satan comes to steal, kill, and destroy. Sin, sickness, disease, poverty, lack, and mental problems come from him. However, James 1:17 says that God gives us every good and perfect thing that we have. There is no variation or shadow of turning in Him. No matter which way we look at Him, there is only light!

"Acts of God"

My homeowner's insurance policy talks about tornadoes, hurricanes, earthquakes, floods, and other natural disasters and calls them "acts of God."

Recently, I was watching a television broadcast about a tornado that destroyed a town in Minnesota and heard the newscaster refer to the storm as an act of God.

Used in that sense, "an act of God" is a term that I hate more than any other expression on earth!

Mark 4 talks about a time when Jesus encountered a storm. Jesus' behavior in the presence of the storm helps us understand where storms originate.

Jesus spent the day sitting in a boat, teaching parables to a crowd of people who had gathered along the shores of the Sea of Galilee. When evening came, He said to His disciples, "Let's go over to the other side of the lake so that I can preach to those people too."

Then He went to the stern of the boat, put His head on a leather cushion, and fell asleep.

The disciples started crossing the lake, but a furious storm of hurricane strength arose and pounded the boat, which began to fill with water. Frightened for their lives, the disciples awoke Jesus.

"Here you are, sleeping!" they cried. "Don't You care that we're drowning? Do You want us to die? Get up and help us!"

Jesus, who had slept undisturbed in the midst of the storm, arose, rebuked the wind, and spoke to the sea. "Hush now!" He said, and the wind sank to rest. Immediately, there was a great calm and perfect peacefulness on the lake.

"Why are you so timid and fearful?" Jesus asked His disciples. "Why do you have no faith? You could have done the same thing I did. You could have calmed the storm."

If this storm had been an act of God, Jesus would have been in conflict with the will of His Father when He calmed the storm, and He would have been encouraging His disciples to resist God's perfect will, too. A division between God and Jesus would have occurred. Since Matthew 12:25 says that a house divided against itself cannot stand, tragedy and destruction would have come.

Instead, Jesus rebuked the storm and brought perfect peacefulness. That's because the storm was not an act of God. It was an act of the enemy, Satan.

God never brings tornadoes, hurricanes, earthquakes, volcanoes, floods, or storms. Satan wants to prevent us from "crossing over to the other side," so he brings these disasters. Our job as believers is to trust God, stay at peace, and order the storm to cease.

Tested by Fire

Often, when we talk about calming storms, we are certain that we know what to do. However, when the storm actually comes, we are tempted to lose our confidence and be afraid.

James 1:12 says, *"Blessed is the man who endureth temptation...."*

In other words, blessed is the man who stands his ground and doesn't move when storms, tests, trials, and infirmities come.

Recently, my family was tested by a storm. Our daughter went away to church camp. Late one night, while my wife and I were sleeping, we got a call from the camp. That day, our daughter had developed chest pain after playing a game of tackle football in the rain, so she had gone to the emergency room. The emergency room doctor believed that her chest pain was caused by a life-threatening heart disease.

My wife and I drove for two and a half hours in the middle of the night to get to our daughter's bedside. I kept thinking, *We will go through all of this, and the doctors will find out that their diagnosis is wrong. They'll realize that my daughter doesn't have anything wrong with her heart.*

As soon as we arrived at the hospital, the doctor who was treating our daughter told us he wanted to keep her in the hospital overnight and then rush her the next morning to a larger hospital so that a heart specialist could examine her. As a way of emphasizing the urgency of her situation, he told us the story of a boy who had recently come into the hospital with a similar heart condition. "He was lying there. I turned around, and the next thing I knew, he was dead. He was blue," the doctor said.

I was astonished that the doctor had said these things in front of my little girl. I knew that he had frightened her. When I looked at her, I could see tears streaming down her face.

I was feeling bombarded too. I said, "I have to go outside for a little while." I found a private place and got into the Presence of the Lord. In the midst of the storm, He gave me perfect peace.

I went back into the hospital and into my daughter's room. My wife and I laid hands on our daughter, prayed for her, and commanded the storm to cease. Then, I said to the doctor, "You can keep her overnight. That's not going to hurt anything." My wife and I stayed in the room with our daughter, and we were so relaxed that we fell asleep.

The next morning, the doctor said, "We're rushing your daughter by ambulance to another hospital."

I said, "That's okay. My wife and I will take her."

We drove our daughter to a hospital where a children's heart specialist examined and tested her. After he reviewed all the tests, he said, "Everything is fine. Don't worry about it. Take her home."

God Brings Life, Not Death

Years ago, I would have been shaken if my daughter had been in an emergency room. I would have been in fear. I probably would have thought, *God, why are You allowing us to go through all this?*

However, I have learned that God does not bring any of this, either directly or indirectly. These things only come to us because of our enemy.

In John 10:10, Jesus says, *"The thief cometh not, but for to steal, and to kill, and to destroy: I am come that they might have LIFE, and that they might have it more abundantly."*

The word "life" is the Greek word "zoë," which means, *an abundant, everlasting, God-kind of life.* It is an earthly existence, yet it is heavenly. Jesus is saying that He didn't come to take your life. He didn't come to trouble you. He came to give you life—exceeding, super-abounding. Whatever you need is what He is willing to bring.

God is Not the Author of Sickness!

God does not bring trouble into our lives. The Bible teaches us that He does not give us sickness, storms, or darkness of any sort.

Occasionally, I talk to people who say, "I don't know why God made me sick. I'm praying about it so that I can find out why He did this to me."

When I hear a comment like that, my heart is grieved. The Word of God is very clear, God doesn't bring sickness. He has provided healing for us, and desires us to walk in health every day of our lives!

CHAPTER TWO

JESUS WANTS YOU TO BE HEALED!

No one in Heaven has colds, headaches, allergies, upset stomachs, or heart disease. God does not pour anything bad on the inhabitants of Heaven, and His Word clearly states that He wants us to be healed too. Jesus says in John 10:10 that He came to give us zoë life, God's heavenly life, which brings deliverance from sickness and infirmity.

We have heard so much about healing that it isn't an exciting message for us anymore. "I already know about healing," we say. And yet our churches are filled with sick believers. Obviously, we don't know everything we need to know about healing, and we need to study it again.

Young's Understanding of Hebrew Scripture

One day, while I was praying, God's Spirit showed me that His people come to church believing that He makes them sick because of verses they have read in the Old Testament.

For example, people read Deuteronomy 28:27 and 28, which says that God smites the disobedient with tumors, hemorrhoids, scurvy, itch, madness, blindness, and dismay of heart from which no man can save them. So, they think, *When people sin, God makes them sick.*

People read Ezekiel 32, which says that God will scatter the Egyptian pharaoh's flesh upon the mountains and darken the sun and stars, and they think, *When nations are carnal, God gives them political upheaval and natural calamity.*

Young's Literal Translation, which was written by a Hebrew scholar, examines these difficult verses by returning to the original Hebrew text.

According to Young and other scholars, the Hebrew language has two tenses—the causative tense and the permissive tense. The *causative* tense is the *active* tense. The subject of the sentence *causes* the action. *The bullet hit the tree. The runaway train ran into the mountainside.* The men who translated the Old Testament from Hebrew to English used the causative tense, so the Old Testament is filled with verses that say, "God did this. God did that. God smote this. God destroyed that."

The *permissive* tense is best translated, "It was allowed." Verses that say, "God causes sickness," have been incorrectly translated. They were originally written in the Hebrew permissive tense and should read, "God *allows* sickness to come."

I know that some people think, *Causative, pausitive. I don't care about any of that.* But, it is important to look at scripture in the proper tense to exact the true meaning.

The Ministry of Jesus

We have already established that sickness, which comes from Satan, entered the world as a result of Adam's sin. A curse hangs over mankind because of Adam's disobedience, and sickness is part of that curse.

There are some that think, *Well, there you are. We're born with a curse hanging over our heads, and as long as we're in this world, we're going to be sick. We may as well accept it, because that's the way it is.*

However, Jesus came to cure the sin problem. Galatians 3:13 says that when He went to Calvary, He redeemed, or repurchased, us: *"Christ hath redeemed us from the curse of the law, being made a curse for us: for it is written, Cursed is every one that hangeth on a tree."* He bought us back from Satan, cleared our debt of sin, bought our freedom from sickness and lack, and set us free.

Healing comes from Jesus and the redemptive work that He did at Calvary.

You may be thinking, *I know that Jesus wants to heal me, so I suppose I've heard all I need to hear on the subject of healing.*

If someone came up to you and asked, "Is it God's will to heal you?" you could say, "Yes, it is God's will to heal me." But could you provide a Scripture to back up your claim? If you have no Scripture, you have no foundation. Instead, you have a little bit of head knowledge that came as a result of something you heard someone say. You're like a table that has only one of its four legs on the floor. It won't take much pressure to topple your belief. In the day of trouble, when sickness knocks on your door, your head knowledge will vanish.

You need a strong foundation, and Scripture builds a foundation that goes deep into the soul.

Jesus—the Exact Image of God

Occasionally, I meet a child who is the mirror image of his parent. He looks and acts exactly like his mom or dad.

The Bible says that Jesus is the exact image of His Father.

Hebrews 1:3 says, *"Who being the brightness of his glory, and the express image of his person..."*

In *The Amplified Bible*, Hebrews 1:3 says, *"He (Jesus) is the sole expression of the glory of God, and He is the perfect imprint and very image of God's nature."*

The Message Bible says, *"The Son perfectly mirrors God and is stamped with God's very nature."*

You and I are not the mirror of God, but Jesus is. John 14:9 says that when you have seen Jesus, you have seen the Father. There is no difference between them. We can find out what God is like by looking at Jesus, because Jesus looks, acts, thinks, and speaks exactly like God.

John 6:38 (NKJV) says, *"For I have come down from Heaven, not to do My own will, but the will of Him who sent Me."*

In other words, Jesus always did exactly what God wanted Him to do. When Jesus healed those who came to Him, God wasn't sitting in Heaven, angry at Jesus for healing people. God was well pleased with His Son because Jesus was imitating the Father and doing exactly what God would do. Jesus said, "Whatever the will of the Father is, that's what I am."

And that's what Hebrews 1:3 is saying. Jesus is the exact expression of God.

Since observing Jesus is the same as looking at God, we can settle the question of whether or not God causes sickness by examining Jesus' ministry.

People often say, "I was too busy. God gave me this illness so that I would slow down and spend time with Him."

Or, "God gave me this crippling disease so that I would learn patience."

Or, "God gave me cancer so that I would learn how to exercise my faith."

But if God gives diseases to people so that they will learn patience, improve their faith walk, or live balanced lives, we would see those things in Jesus' ministry.

If God punishes disobedient or carnal people by giving them diseases, Jesus would give them diseases too. After all, Jesus does exactly what God would do.

Did Jesus ever go to the synagogue on the Sabbath day and say, "All of you who want to have more patience, come up to the altar. I will lay hands on you and give you painful, crippling diseases that will put you in wheelchairs so that you can bear the spiritual fruit of patience"?

Did He ever say to the people who gathered around Him, "Some of you have not been spending enough time in your prayer closets. You know who you are. Come forward. I will pray for you and give you Chronic Fatigue Syndrome so that you are forced to simplify your schedule and have more time for prayer"?

When He was walking through the marketplace, did Jesus ever go up to someone and say, "You are carnal, and I command the birds of the heavens to gnaw away at your flesh. I give you boils, scurvy, blindness, and madness because I want to punish you for your sin"?

Certainly, Jesus was displeased with the Jewish religious leaders of His day. They had missed their visitation, and He called them blind men and hypocrites. But did He ever say to one of them, "You are a scourge to the people of God. I give you AIDS and leprosy"?

If God were the author of sickness, then He would have worked through Jesus to curse people and give them illnesses.

You might say, "Well, okay. God would never use Jesus to bring sickness, curses, or infirmity. But He sometimes uses the devil to make me sick."

Does God think that an occasional tragedy is good for you? Does He call Satan on the telephone and hire him to torment you? Of course not!

James 1:13 instructs us not to blame God. "Don't ever say that God is using another agent to make you sick." This needs to be settled in your heart. Imposing sickness on you, either directly or indirectly, is not part of God's behavior or strategy.

Religious people often say, "Maybe we don't see any evidence of it in Jesus' ministry, but God makes us sick. Just turn back to the Old Testament and look at the life of Job."

However, God did not make Job sick! Job got into fear, which opened the door for Satan, and *Satan* brought sickness and tragedy into Job's life.

In the Book of Job, Satan comes to God and says, "What about Job?"

God responds, "Job has integrity."

The first three chapters of Job clearly show that Satan wanted to destroy Job's integrity by causing him to lose his faith in God. Certainly, at a moment of great loss, Job wavered. He said, "God is shooting His fiery darts. He is doing these awful things. He prospered me, and now He has taken my blessings away."

Sometimes, when we are upset, we say things we don't really mean. When Job was overwhelmed by loss, he said some things that did not reflect the deepest beliefs of his soul. However, at the end of the Book of Job, God says that Job's heart never turned against Him. In his heart, Job never blamed God or lost his faith.

Yet people quote Job 1:21 at funerals and other times of loss, and believe that it's the Bible's explanation for life's tragedies. "The Lord hath given, and the Lord hath taken away."

But the Lord does not take away. He looks for ways to bless.

If sickness and loss ever knock on your door, resist the temptation to say, "God is bringing this tragedy."

Instead, say, "I don't know everything about this storm, but here is the one thing I do know. It's not God's will for me to be overwhelmed by this situation. It's God's will to heal and deliver me."

Jesus and the Leper

Mark 1:40 illustrates the attitude that many believers have. A leper comes to Jesus, gets on his knees, and begs for help. He says, "I don't know if You are willing to heal me of this incurable leprosy, but if You are willing, You are able to make me clean."

If it were God's will for people to be sick, Jesus would have said to the leper, "I can't heal you. It's not My will to heal you."

Instead, Jesus was moved with compassion. He put forth His hand, touched the leper, and said to him, "I am willing. Be made clean."

As soon as Jesus spoke, leprosy departed from the sick man, and he was cleansed.

"If it be Thy Will"

People often pray this way: "If it be Thy will, take away my cancer. If it be Thy will, deliver my child from Attention Deficit Disorder [ADD]. If it be Thy will, deliver my husband from alcoholism. If it be Thy will..."

The Bible says that God is love. The Bible says that God wants you to live until you are completely satisfied. Does it then make sense for Him to take you to Heaven when you are still needed on earth? Of course not! It makes sense for Him to heal you and fill you with His glory, and that's what He wants to do.

For example, Matthew 4:23 and 24 says, "*And Jesus went about all Galilee, teaching in their synagogues and preaching the gospel of the kingdom, and healing ALL manner of sickness and ALL manner of disease among the people, and His fame went throughout all Syria; and those which were possessed with devils and those which were lunatick, and those that had the palsy; and He healed them.*"

This was a large crowd. If it had been God's will to heal some, but not all, then Jesus would have said to some of them, "I am sorry, but I can't heal everyone. I will heal some but not all. I'm not going to heal you today. Come back tomorrow. It's a 'chance' thing with God. Perhaps I will heal you then."

However, Jesus was a healing Savior, and He served a good and merciful God. He healed each one who came.

Matthew 8:16 presents a similar account: *"When the even was come, they brought unto Him many that were possessed with devils; and He cast out the spirits with His word, and healed all that were sick."*

He didn't say to anyone, "God has given you this illness to teach you a lesson, so I am not going to heal you." No, He healed everyone.

Matthew 15:29 and 30 says, *"And Jesus departed from thence, and came nigh unto the Sea of Galilee; and went up into a mountain, and sat down there. And great multitudes came unto Him, having with them those that were lame, blind, dumb, maimed, and many others, and cast them down at Jesus' feet, and He healed them."*

If it had not been God's will to heal, Jesus would have said, "Maybe I can heal one or two of you, but I can't heal you all."

However, Jesus healed all of them.

The Disciples and the Seventy

Jesus healed everyone who came to Him in simple faith, believing in Him. And He empowered His followers to heal sickness too. Matthew 10:1 says, *"And when He had called unto Him His twelve disciples, He gave them power against unclean spirits, to cast them out, and to heal all manner of sickness and all manner of disease."*

In Matthew 10:8, Jesus says, *"Heal the sick, cleanse the lepers, raise the dead, cast out devils: freely ye have received, freely give."*

When the New Testament was written, leprosy was a prevalent, deadly disease, much like cancer is today. And it was contagious, so people were afraid of lepers and confined them to leper colonies. But Jesus said, "Cleanse those who have leprosy."

Luke 9:1 is an account of the same incident. It says, *"Then he called his twelve disciples together, and gave them power and authority over all devils, and to cure diseases."*

Religious tradition says that healing power was limited to the Twelve and left the Church when the last apostle died. Religion says that Jesus' followers are no longer empowered to cure diseases, but Luke 10 says that Jesus appointed "another seventy" to go ahead of Him into the cities where He would minister. The Seventy also were empowered to heal the sick.

We do not know the names of the Seventy. They were not born again on the inside because Jesus had not yet died on the Cross. But they believed that Jesus was the Messiah, so they were saved under the terms of their covenant, and they received the same power that the disciples received. They are a symbol of what Jesus wants to do through His Church.

In Luke 10:9, Jesus says to the Seventy, *"...heal the sick that are therein, and say unto them, The kingdom of God is come nigh unto you."*

Later in Luke 10, the Seventy return to Jesus with joy, saying, "Lord, it's awesome. Even the devils are subject unto us through Your Name."

However, Jesus says, *"...I beheld Satan as lightning fall from heaven. Behold, I give unto you power to tread on serpents and scorpions, and over all the power of the enemy: and nothing shall by any means hurt you. Notwithstanding in this rejoice not, that the spirits are subject unto you; but rather rejoice, because your names are written in heaven"* (Luke 10:18-20).

Since the Seventy were able to exercise dominion and power, the Church certainly should rise up and do the same. Too often people in the Church are not convinced that God wants to heal and deliver them, and they certainly do not believe that He wants us to bring healing to someone else.

They say, "Jesus gave power to the people who followed Him while He was on earth, but we don't have that kind of power today."

However, when Jesus says, in Luke 10:19, "Behold, I give unto you power," He is talking to the Seventy, but He also is describing the Church.

Power to Destroy the Work of the Enemy

Luke 10:19 makes two references to power. It says, *"Behold, I give unto you POWER to tread on serpents and scorpions, and over all the POWER of the enemy: and nothing shall by any means hurt you."*

In English, we use the same word in both parts of the verse, but the Greek language uses two different words. The first word is "exousia," which means, *delegated influence* or *delegated authority*. The second word is "dunamis," which means, *strength and might*.

"Dunamis" is *mighty, explosive, miracle-working power.* It manifests in Mark 9 when Jesus is transfigured before Peter, James, and John.

"Exousia" is *the power that comes from a higher authority.*

The enemy has a few muscles. Luke 10:19 talks about the power of the enemy. Satan knows how to intimidate wavering Christians. However, Jesus is much greater and mightier than Satan, and He has given us the authority to subdue the enemy.

Unfortunately, we sometimes act like the timid little sheriff's deputy, Barney Fife. Instead of locking up the bad guys, Barney panics and gets locked up by *them*!

Jesus has given us a badge and a gun, so to speak, and we need to learn how to use our *exousia*, or God-given authority. We need to be like the police officer who holds up his badge and says to the criminal, "I have this badge, and you will listen to me." We need to be like the sheriff's deputy who uses his gun to subdue the enemy.

When the devil says, "I am going to give you a headache," we need to say, "In Jesus' Name, I don't want a headache."

When Satan says, "I'm going to give you cancer," we need to say, "I don't want cancer. I don't want one cell of that disease. I am going to live a full life for God and serve Him all of my days. Cancer, get off my body in Jesus' Name."

In Mark 16:15, Jesus tells His disciples to *"...Go ye into all the world, and preach the gospel to every creature."* Most twenty-first century Christians don't wonder about whether or not we should preach the Gospel. We realize

that God sent Jesus to the Cross in order to save
and that He still wants everyone to be saved.

However, we stumble over Mark 16:17
which says, *"And these signs shall follow them that believe; In
my name shall they cast out devils; they shall speak with new
tongues; They shall take up serpents; and if they drink any deadly thing, it shall not hurt them; they shall lay hands on the sick,
and they shall recover."*

We say, "Well, I don't know if it's God's will to heal
everyone." We believe that salvation is still God's will for
everyone, but our philosophy and religion have taught us
to believe that healing is not available to all.

"I grew up in a certain church," some say, "and my
church doesn't believe in healing."

Or, "I don't care what that preacher says. He doesn't
know what he's talking about. My grandparents and parents believed that God makes people sick, and I believe it
too."

However, we do not serve a God who makes people
sick, and we do not serve a God who has taken healing
away. Healing, like salvation, is meant for everyone. It is
available to all.

Faith Doesn't Wait!

Often, I meet people who are waiting for their healing. They are waiting for a man or woman to pray for them,
or for a special preacher to come to town and lay his hands
on them. They are like the man in John chapter 5, who had
been lying beside the pool of Bethesda in Jerusalem for thir-
ty-eight years, hoping to be healed.

He said, "When the waters ripple, I have no man to put me in the pool, and someone always steps ahead of me and is healed. Someone needs to put me in the pool. *I am waiting for a man"*(v. 7).

Often, when we seek healing, we are like the man beside the pool. We are waiting for a man. However, we don't receive our healing because of another person. We receive our healing by our faith.

Jesus said to the man by the pool, *"...Rise, take up thy bed, and walk"* (John 5:8). Because the man had faith in Jesus and acted on his faith, he was healed.

Faith Doesn't Deny the Problem

Sometimes, people get confused about acting on faith. They don't know what it means. They think that to act in faith means to deny the symptom or problem.

Faith does not deny the existence of natural symptoms. If a man cannot see without his glasses, he doesn't necessarily say, "I'm healed. I don't need my glasses anymore," and then throw away his glasses. While he is still wearing his glasses, he should say, "I don't care what the natural realm says. I'm going to believe what the Bible says. I'm already healed in Jesus' Name. The healing power of God is working in my eyes right now. Glory to God, I release healing power in Jesus' Name."

Here's the problem with many church people: Instead of saying, "I'm healed," they'll either deny the existence of the sickness or they'll say, "Well, I don't know if I'm healed or not."

Exercising Faith

If sickness comes, we need to exercise our faith, and exercising faith is a lot like exercising the body.

In the summer between eighth and ninth grade, I was a skinny, 109 pound little guy. But I wanted to play football, so I said to my older brother, Joe, "I want to be like you. I want to be strong." So Joe taught me how to lift weights.

After I worked out for the first time, I looked in the mirror, hoping to see a change, but everything looked the same. I did not get immediate results, but since I had begun to exercise, change had begun to occur. If I had become discouraged and quit, I would never have experienced a dramatic change in my body.

However, day after day, I continued to work out and do what my brother told me to do. After awhile, my muscles began to respond to persistent exercise. In fact, I changed so much in the summer between the ninth and tenth grade that people hardly recognized me when I returned to school.

People want to exercise their faith and get immediate results. Usually, however, exercising faith is like exercising muscles. You may not see a change right away, but if you continue to exercise daily, you will eventually see good results.

Weak faith is like weak muscles. It may not have much impact at first, but if you begin to exercise it, it will gain strength.

If you say to your sickness, "By the stripes of Jesus, I am healed [1 Peter 2:24]," you may not see an immediate change, but if you say it every morning, day after day, your faith will grow, and healing will come.

Jesus is the exact image of His Father. While He was on the earth, He did exactly what God would do. Jesus healed everyone who came to Him, and He empowered His followers to bring healing too. However, we don't receive healing because of another person. We receive our healing because of our faith. When we use our faith, healing comes.

CHAPTER THREE

OLD TESTAMENT TYPES AND SHADOWS

We don't live under the regulations of the Old Testament. We have liberty from the Old Covenant. According to Hebrews 8:6, through Jesus' death, resurrection, and ascension to Heaven, He established a better covenant, and that New Covenant is established on better promises.

Old Testament Scripture was written for our instruction. Hebrews 10:1 says that the Law is an outline, or foreshadowing, of all the good things that come with the New Covenant.

Old Testament Scripture contains patterns and examples that reveal the truth. We refer to Old Testament Scripture as "types and shadows," and we find healing in the types and shadows of the Old Testament.

Throughout the Old Testament, God is a healing God, and New Testament believers have a *better* covenant that is established on *better* promises. We have to wonder why God healed people for approximately four thousand years and then, according to some Christians, became a God of sickness and infirmity when He established a better covenant!

Old Testament Names for God

God has several names in the Old Testament. These names reveal who He is and describe distinct aspects of His personality.

For example, God is frequently called Jehovah Jireh, our Provider. Another Old Testament name for God is Jehovah Rapha, the Lord Your Healer, the God who heals. The Hebrew language says that He is *the One who "stitches you up and makes you whole."*

A third Old Testament name for God is El Shaddai. The literal meaning of El Shaddai is *the "breasty one"* or *the One who nourishes you at His breast.* People usually don't want to talk about this aspect of God's personality because it suggests breastfeeding, but the Hebrew language paints this picture of El Shaddai: A woman's child comes to her, and she gives him everything he needs by feeding him at her breast. She supplies everything. She is the "breasty one."

Several years ago, I became so interested in the meaning of El Shaddai that I studied breastfeeding. I learned that the mother does not get milk right away. Typically, she gets milk on the third postpartum day. For the first two or three days of his life, the baby receives a substance called colostrum when he nurses. This thin, yellowish fluid contains many proteins, calories, and antibodies. It is so rich and nourishing that it has been described as "the fountain of life."

Colostrum is so beneficial to babies that mothers who are planning to bottle-feed are encouraged to nurse their children for the first two or three days. The baby's immune system is immature, but colostrum, which gives babies an immediate, supercharged dose of the mother's antibodies, prevents infection and protects them from illness. It causes sickness and disease to stay far away.

We can draw a lot of analogies between the two days (two thousand years) of the Church Age and the two days when the mother provides colostrum to the newborn child. Surely, as part of His redemptive work, Jesus offers His Church a spiritual substance that protects us from illness and keeps sickness far away.

God is everything we need! When we need a father, He is a father; but when we need a mother, He is a mother too. He is El Shaddai, the "breasty one." When hungry baby Christians feed on the milk of God's Word, God surely must give them "first milk" so that His own substance, His own invulnerability to the curse of the enemy, flows into their lives.

The Value of the Old Testament

Our country has people who live and work in New York and California. These people don't spend much time in the middle of the country. They get a glimpse of mid-America as they travel by air from one coast to the other and refer to it as "flyover territory."

Sometimes, as Christians, we think of the Old Testament as "flyover territory," *No need to stop here.*

Certainly, we don't want to go back and live in the Old Testament. Thank God, we no longer need to observe the strict rules about the Passover Supper or make sure that our Saturday evening meals are ceremonially clean. Jesus has given us liberty from Old Testament regulations.

However, the New Testament makes it clear that Old Testament events are our examples and that we benefit by studying them.

Romans 15:4 says, *"For whatsoever things were written aforetime were written for our learning* [our instruction]*, that we through patience and comfort of the scriptures might have hope."* In the Book of Exodus, Moses brings the children of Israel out of Egypt, leads them through the Red Sea, and takes them through the wilderness by following the glory cloud. First Corinthians 10 talks about the events of Exodus. Verse 6 says, *"Now these things were our examples* [warnings and admonitions]*, to the intent we should not lust after evil* [carnal] *things, as they also lusted."*

Verses 7 through 10 list Israel's mistakes. The Israelites worshipped false gods, gratified evil desires, tempted the Lord, exploited His goodness, and murmured against Him. They left Egypt, but that generation never entered the Promised Land. They wandered in the wilderness for the rest of their lives and were finally put out of the way by death.

First Corinthians 10:11 says, *"Now all these things happened unto them for ensamples* [as warnings to us]*: and they are written for our admonition* [to equip us for right action by good instruction]*, upon whom the ends of the world are come* [those who live in the days when the climax of the ages comes]*."*

We can learn from the children of Israel. God does not want us to spend our born-again lives in the "wilderness." He wants us to pass through the wilderness and get to our Promised Land. He has given us types and shadows in the Old Testament so that we can learn from the Israelites and not make the same mistakes.

Jesus as the One Who Completes the Old Covenant

John 3:14 says, *"And as Moses lifted up the serpent in the wilderness, even so must the Son of man be lifted up."*

This verse is not in our Bibles by mistake. When it talks about the serpent in the wilderness, it refers to an Old Testament foreshadowing or *type*.

We think of the four Gospels, Matthew, Mark, Luke, and John, as New Testament Books, and, certainly, they belong in the New Testament. They are portraits of the life of Christ. However, the Gospels do not become New Testament Books until Jesus suffers on the Cross. We do not see the New Covenant in operation until we get to the Book of Acts.

Throughout His ministry on earth, Jesus was in the process of bringing in the New Covenant, but He was still functioning under the Law. He was fulfilling Old Testament types.

We see healing in the Old Testament when we study its shadows and types.

The Bronze Serpent—an Old Testament Type

John 3:14 refers to an Old Testament event that is described in Numbers 21.

Israel is traveling through the wilderness. Arad, a southern Canaanite king, hears that Israel is coming toward his country and instructs his army to attack Israel. The Canaanite army takes Israelite prisoners, so the Israelites make a vow to God. They say, "If You will give us the Canaanites, we will completely destroy their cities."

God allows the Israelites to have domination over the Canaanites, and Israel destroys Arad's cities. The Israelites enjoy a great victory.

However, as they journey from southern Canaan to the Red Sea, the Israelites become impatient, discouraged, and depressed because of the trials they encounter. They begin to complain against God and Moses. They say in Numbers 21:5, "Why have you brought us out of Egypt to die in the wilderness? For there is no bread, neither is there water, and we loathe this light, contemptible, unsubstantial manna."

God has used Moses to subdue the powerful Egyptian pharaoh and has delivered the Israelites from slavery. He has given them a miraculous military victory over a well-armed Canaanite army. Yet they complain to Him, so God allows fiery, burning serpents to attack the Israelites, and many Israelites die.

Old Testament verses that talk about the Israelites are always written in the permissive tense. God does not send fiery serpents, but God allows the serpents to come.

People often say, "Deadly, stinging, hissing snakes, why does God allow these things?"

The answer is found in God's attitude toward covenants.

God is always faithful to His Word, so when He forms a covenant, He honors it. When He made a covenant with Abraham, He said, "If you will obey Me, I will bless you." He warned Abraham and His descendants that they would lose their victory if they walked outside the covenant, but He gave them the power to choose their own way.

According to the covenant God formed with Israel, He couldn't stop the hissing snakes. The Israelites violated their covenant with God, and Satan had the legal right to bring them cursing and death.

Through the redemptive work of Jesus, we have a better covenant, but if we neglect our salvation and allow a pattern of sin to take root in our lives, we will get into trouble too. Of course, when the enemy touches us, we can say, "No, I bind you in Jesus' Name." But we also need to repent. Repentance allows God's mercy to flow into our lives.

In Numbers 21:7, the people of Israel repented. They said to Moses, "We have sinned by speaking against the Lord and you," and Moses prayed for them. When the Israelites repented, God had the legal right to move in their lives again.

God told Moses to make a bronze serpent and set it on a pole. God said, "...*every one that is bitten, when he looketh upon it, shall live.*"

We are very blessed; we live in the light of the Word. We don't have to hear the Word from someone else in order to understand it. We are able to read it for ourselves. We can bring something over from the Old Testament, put it in the light, and realize what it means.

The people of Israel, however, were living under a shadow. This was not the *shadow of the Almighty*, which is a place of protection that is talked about in Psalm 91:1. The Israelites lived under a shadow that cast darkness. They did not understand the Word of God, so God would reveal His Word to a king, priest, or prophet, and the king, priest, or prophet would explain the Word to the people.

The bronze serpent in Numbers 21 is a symbol, or a *type*. The serpent on the pole represents Jesus on the Cross, and the pole is a type of the Cross.

When the Israelites looked upon the bronze serpent, they were healed of their sicknesses. They were made whole. Their experience was a foreshadowing of Jesus' redemptive work on the Cross.

Interestingly, when we look at the Cross, we usually think about salvation. We don't think about healing, but the Cross brings healing too.

Redemption means, *ransom in full.* It is salvation *and* healing. Jesus died to save people from hell, but He also died to restore them and make them new. When the Israelites looked at the bronze serpent, they were healed. If you look at Jesus on the Cross, you will be healed too.

The Passover Lamb

In Exodus 12:3, God says to Moses, *"...take to them* [the congregation of Israel] *every man a lamb, according to the house of their fathers, a lamb for an house."*

This was to be a lamb without blemish.

God said, "Cut up that lamb. Eat the flesh of the lamb and put its blood upon your doorposts and your lintel. For I am passing through Egypt tonight, and I will judge every household that does not have the lamb's blood on its doorpost, and then the Death Angel will come. But when I see the blood of the lamb on your doorposts, I will not allow the destroyer to come into your house to smite you. I will pass over your house."

First Corinthians 5:7 brings the Passover lamb into the New Testament. It says, "Christ is our Passover

Lamb, and He has been sacrificed."In other words, the Passover lamb is an Old Testament type of Jesus' work on the Cross.

In John 6:53 and 54, Jesus tells us to eat His flesh and drink His blood, and we usually think of Communion when we hear these verses, but the Lord's Supper is only the ceremonial side of the verse. John 1:14 says that the Word "was made flesh and dwelt among us." And when Jesus tells us to eat His flesh and drink His blood, He is referring to the Word. He is telling us to eat the Word, the way the Israelites ate the Passover lamb, so that it gets on the inside of us where it can give us life. He is also telling us to drink the blood, which has power to protect, so that His protection from judgment and destruction can come.

Jesus, our Passover Lamb, through His flesh and blood, provides two things: protection and healing.

Making Much of the Blood

"The Old Testament was too bloody," some people say. "I don't want a bloody Gospel. I don't want to sing songs about the power of the blood, and I don't want to hear sermons about it. I want to have a bloodless Christianity."

Jesus shed His blood, so we don't have to shed blood today. But Revelation 12:11 says that our enemy will be overcome by the word of our testimony *and* by the blood of the Lamb, so the Bible places great value on the blood.

Some people complain when we plead the blood of Jesus in our prayers. "Pleading the blood is not in the

Bible," they say. However, the Bible talks about the blood. For example, Matthew 26:28 says that the blood of Jesus was shed for the *remission* of sin. In other words, at the moment we are born again, we are delivered from our sins because of Jesus' shed blood.

Romans 3:25 says that we are redeemed through *faith* in the blood, which means that we can only know Jesus if we are willing to trust in the power and value of His blood.

The Old Testament says, "Put some blood around your doorpost, and when the angel of destruction comes by, the blood will keep him away from your family."

That's an exciting concept for me. If we make much of the blood in our homes, when the devil comes with destruction, he sees the blood and leaves our homes alone.

When a tornado comes, it will pass over our house if we make much of the blood. When the tornado sees the blood on our doorposts, it says, "I need to pass over that place."

The destroyer will also pass over when we make much of the blood in our schools. When we pray, "My children are covered and protected by the blood. This is a blood-bought school," then crazy devils won't come into our children's schools to provoke rebellion and violence.

Don't put the blood into a corner of your Christian life. Make much of the blood. The blood of Jesus redeemed you, and you are protected by it. The blood is the way that healing comes to you.

The Water at Marah

Exodus 15:23-25 says, *"And when they came to Marah, they could not drink of the waters of Marah, for they were bitter: And the people murmured against Moses, saying, 'What shall we drink?' And he cried unto the Lord, and the Lord shewed him a tree, which when he had cast into the waters, the waters were made sweet..."*

In the Old Testament, waters represent multitudes of people. The tree that Moses threw into the water in Exodus 15 is a type of Jesus on the Cross. When the multitudes are drawn to Jesus on the Cross, they get saved, and salvation changes their lives from bitter to sweet.

Perhaps you're thinking, *Well, I got saved, and I don't have a sweet life. I'm going through a lot of things right now. I'm living in hell on earth.*

Perhaps you are facing great difficulty, but you are not in hell. Hell is much worse than most of us comprehend. In hell, people weep in unspeakable anguish as worms come out of their mouths and ears. They cry out to the Savior they rejected on earth. In fact, they bow their knee every day and say, "Jesus is Lord." But bowing in hell does not bring deliverance. It only brings the torment of regret. There's no purgatory, no praying people out. Hell is an unspeakable punishment, and Jesus died to rescue us from hell.

But, salvation isn't the only promise revealed at Marah. Verse 26 goes on to say that, *"If thou wilt diligently hearken to THE VOICE OF THE LORD THY GOD, and wilt do that which is right in his sight, and wilt give ear to his commandments, and keep all his statutes, I will put none of these diseases upon thee, which I have brought upon the Egyptians: for I am the Lord that healeth thee."*

If we are going to hearken to "the voice of the Lord thy God," then we must read His Holy written Word. His Word is God directly speaking to us.

The next part of that verse, "...and wilt do that which is right in his sight..." means living holy and walking in God. And "...wilt give ear to his commandments, and keep all his statutes..." means doing what He tells you to do.

In other words, if you will diligently hearken to the Word and will live holy, walking in God, and if you will do what He tells you to do, He will not allow the diseases that come to unsaved people to come upon you, for He is the Lord who heals you of your diseases.

Nowhere in Scripture does God say, "I am the God that killeth thee." He never says, "I am the God that maketh thee sick." However, in Exodus 15:26, He does say, "If you will accept Me, I am the God that healeth thee."

Don't Lose God's Benefits!

We see, then, that the Old Testament contains types and shadows, and these types and shadows teach us that Jesus died to save us from hell and to heal our sicknesses. The bronze serpent, the Passover lamb, and the tree in the waters of Marah are types of Jesus' ministry, and they tie healing and salvation together.

Psalm 103:2 says, "Bless the Lord, O my soul, and forget not all His benefits."

In this verse, the word "forget" means, to mislay. Mislaying one of God's benefits is like losing your car keys or leaving your wallet in the cart at the grocery store. In other words, if you lost these things, you'd need to go back and look for them.

Psalm 103:3 talks about God's benefits. It lists two things. It says that God forgives all of our iniquities and *heals all of our diseases.* Why is it that we are able to embrace the idea that God wants to forgive all of our iniquities, but we can't quite believe that He wants to heal our diseases? We keep up with salvation, but like the lost wallet, we leave healing behind in the cart at the grocery store. We need to find it. We need to go back to the place where we lost healing and get it back again.

CHAPTER FOUR

HEALING WAS PAID FOR ON THE CROSS

Because of Jesus' death, resurrection, and ascension, we have been delivered from the power and dominion of sin, and if salvation had been the only aspect of Jesus' redemptive work, we would have much to celebrate. However, salvation is not the only thing that Jesus provided for us when He died. When He purchased our salvation, He paid for our healing too.

Some churches are passionate about salvation, but it is the only part of the redemptive plan they accept. They don't believe in healing or prosperity. "We only believe in salvation," they say. You might say that they take enough of Jesus to stay out of hell, but they don't receive enough of Him to live in victory.

Eternity in Heaven is wonderful, but it is not the only thing that the plan of redemption provides. The Bible says that at the same time Jesus bought our deliverance from sin and death, He also redeemed us from sickness and poverty.

Second Corinthians 5:17 says, "...*if any man be IN CHRIST, he is a new creature: old things are passed away; behold, all things are become new.*"

In other words, when we are born again, we relocate from a place of cursing and death to a place in Christ, and we become a new man. Old things are passed away. Behold, *all* things are become new!

On the inside, the old sin nature is removed and a brand-new man is formed.

Second Corinthians 5:21 says, "*For he* [God] *hath made him* [Jesus] *to be sin for us, who knew no sin; that we might be made the righteousness of God in him.*"

Healing: Another Free Gift

The good news of the Gospel is that you don't have to be sick. Healing is a free gift, provided to you by God through Jesus, even as righteousness is a free gift.

Romans 3:22 says, "*Even the righteousness of God which is by faith of Jesus Christ unto all and upon all them that believe...*"

Righteousness is *right standing with God.* Romans 3:22 tells us that right standing is a free gift for anyone who has faith in Jesus Christ.

Often, people make the mistake of thinking they have to earn their right standing with God. They work for salvation, and if they get sick, they strive for healing too.

Romans 3:24 says, "*Being justified freely by his grace through the redemption that is in Christ Jesus.*"

Justified means *to render someone righteous* or *to render someone innocent.*

Romans 3:24 does not tell us that we are rendered innocent by our own efforts. This verse tells us that we are rendered innocent by His grace. We didn't earn righteousness, but we get it anyway. This is good news! We get it for free. Romans 3:26 says that Jesus renders to us righteousness when we believe.

Does it make sense that God was willing to send His Son to the Cross to purchase your righteousness, but did not want to buy your healing? Does it make sense for God to say, "You can be righteous, but you can't be healed. Although I saved you from sin and hell, I did not save you from sickness and disease. You will still have the same sicknesses that you had before"?

Of course it doesn't make sense! God's Son purchased your righteousness, and He purchased your healing too. Healing and righteousness are part of the same redemptive plan.

We often think that healing is a complicated process. But healing, like righteousness, is a free gift that comes totally from God. The only thing you have to do to be healed is believe the Word.

Purchased to be Released

As I said, righteousness means, *right standing with God*. Redemption, another word that is used throughout the Bible, means, *to liberate by payment* or *to pay a ransom so that a captured person can be released*.

When you redeem someone, you make a payment to get him back.

Through His shed blood, Jesus redeemed you and me. He paid a ransom so that we could be released from the captivity of sin.

Each portion of our captivity required a different payment. First Peter 2:24 says that Jesus paid for our healing with His stripes. He paid for our healing when He was flogged. The Roman army put thirty-nine stripes on Jesus' back, and I don't think it's a coincidence that physicians have discovered thirty-nine different divisions of sickness and disease. With the thirty-nine lashes He received, Jesus purchased our redemption from thirty-nine categories of disease.

That the Blessings Might be Ours

You and I were cursed, and Jesus went to the Cross and paid the ransom so that we could be set free from the curse.

Galatians 3:13 tells us that *"Christ* [the Anointing, the Anointed One] *hath redeemed us from the curse of the law, being made a curse for us: for it is written, Cursed is every one that hangeth on a tree."*

Different translations of Galatians 3:13 help us to understand the verse.

The *Wade Translation* says, *"Now Christ bought us from the curse of the law at the cost of being accursed for our sake."*

The *Twentieth Century Translation* says, *"Christ ransomed us from the curse pronounced in the law."*

The *Translator's Translation* says, *"Christ redeemed us from the curse of the law by taking the curse upon himself."*

Galatians 3:14 goes on to say, *"that through their receiving Christ Jesus, the blessing promised to Abraham might come upon the Gentiles."*

Abraham had Isaac, the son of promise, and Isaac had sons. Isaac's descendants were the children of Israel, and God bestowed great blessings on them. Deuteronomy 28 says that blessing overtook them when they obeyed the Lord. God gave them a "surplus of prosperity" and protected them from the deadly diseases that caused other nations to suffer.

If we are in Christ, we are the spiritual seed of Abraham, and all of the blessings that God gave the children of Israel are available to us. Galatians 3:14 says, *"That the blessing of Abraham MIGHT come..."* Those blessings won't come to us if we do not accept them, but they are ours if we receive them by faith.

Scriptural Proof That Healing is Part of Redemption

Isaiah 53 describes the ministry of Jesus Christ. In the *King James Version*, Isaiah 53:4 says, *"Surely he hath borne our griefs, and carried our sorrows..."* You probably are familiar with this verse, but you may not know that it is translated inaccurately.

The Hebrew word "choliy" is used in Isaiah 53:4. It is translated "griefs," but it actually means, *malady or disease*. It is used twenty other times in the Old Testament, and in those twenty verses, it is translated "sickness" or "disease."

For example, "choliy" is used in Deuteronomy 7:15, which says, *"And the Lord will take away from thee all sickness* [choliy], *and will put none of the evil diseases of Egypt, which thou knowest, upon thee...*"

It is also used in Deuteronomy 28:59, where God warns the Israelites that disobedience would make them vulnerable to plagues and *sicknesses.*

It is used again in 1 Kings 17, where Elijah prayed for the widow's child after the boy got sick and died. Interestingly, the only place in the Old Testament where the word "choliy" is translated "griefs" is in Isaiah 53.

The word "sorrow" in Isaiah 53:4 is also mistranslated. This word, which is used four or five other times in the Old Testament, means *pain.* In fact, the *Jerusalem Bible* does not even list "sorrow" as a secondary meaning, and when it is used in other Old Testament verses, such as Job 33:19 and Jeremiah 51:8, it is always translated "pain."

However, in Isaiah 53:4, it is translated "sorrow," which is not an accurate translation.

The scholars who translated the Old Testament for King James were not born-again believers, and, occasionally, they gave their own interpretation to Bible verses. When they read Isaiah 53:4 in the Hebrew language, they must have thought, *There's no way that Jesus could have paid for sickness and pain. We can't use those words. We'll say something else so that the verses line up with a more traditional interpretation of Christianity.*

However, because we have a clearer understanding of the character of God, we know that the translation of Isaiah 53:4,5 should read, *"Surely he hath borne our griefs* (sicknesses) *and carried our sorrows* (pains); *yet we did esteem him stricken, smitten of God, and afflicted. But, He was wounded for our transgressions, he was bruised for our iniquities; the chastisement of our peace was upon him, and with his stripes we are healed."*

When these verses are translated accurately, they show that Jesus died to accomplish two things: to provide forgiveness and cleansing of sin *and* to provide healing of physical sickness or disease.

When Jesus was wounded for our transgressions and bruised for our iniquities, He was dealing with our sin.

However, Isaiah 53:5 also says, *"...the chastisement of our peace was upon Him, and with his stripes we are healed."* In this part of the verse, Jesus is not dealing with our sin. He is dealing with our sickness and disease.

According to Isaiah 53, Jesus saves us, and then He heals us.

Of course, Isaiah, who is an Old Testament prophet, is talking about future events. And in Matthew 8:16 and 17, Jesus fulfills Isaiah's prophecy. The verses say, *"When the even was come, they brought unto him many that were possessed with devils; and he cast out the spirits with his word, and healed all that were sick; that it might be fulfilled which was spoken by Esaias the prophet, saying, Himself took our infirmities, and bare our sicknesses."*

People often say, "Jesus heals the spirit. That's the healing that Isaiah 53 is referring to." However Matthew 8 says that Jesus fulfilled, or completed, Isaiah's prophecy by healing the physical sicknesses of those who came to Him.

Mark chapter 2 also indicates that Jesus came to accomplish forgiveness of sin *and* healing of disease. A paralytic is brought to Jesus, and when Jesus sees the man's faith, He says, "Your sins are forgiven and put away."

Some scribes are there, and they began to think, *Who does this man think He is, offering forgiveness to someone? That's blasphemy!*

Jesus knows what the scribes are thinking, so He turns to them and says, "What is easier? Is it easier to tell a paralyzed man that his sins are forgiven, or is it easier to say, 'Rise, take up your sleeping mat, and walk?'"

"But so that you will know beyond a doubt that the Son of Man has the right and authority to forgive sins, I say to this man, 'Get up and walk.'"

Of course, the paralyzed man doesn't stop to think. Immediately, he gets up, grabs his mat, and walks away.

I love Jesus' boldness. In this story, He indicates that He has two areas of authority—the authority to forgive and remove sin, and the authority to heal.

The Icing on the Cake

Where healing is concerned, I like to think of the New Testament Book of James, which was written after Jesus' crucifixion, as "the icing on the cake." It confirms everything that we have already read.

James, the Book's author, was the naturally born son of Joseph and Mary, so he was Jesus' half brother. At first, James did not believe in Jesus' ministry, according to John 7:5. Later, however, he was born again, and he became the pastor of a Jewish church.

You might think, *James had special privileges. Whatever promises James writes about are meant for the privileged few.* However, James addresses his Book to Christians in general.

In James 5:13, he writes, *"Is any among you afflicted? let him pray. Is any merry? let him sing psalms."*

In this verse, James tells us what to do when we are afflicted, under pressure, suffering a hardship, and feeling like giving up.

You may notice that James does *not* instruct us to call the pastor on the telephone and tell him all about our trouble and affliction, and he does not tell us to become offended if the pastor and other members of the church do not figure out that we are having a bad time.

Instead, he tells us to pray. Of course, church members should have compassion for one another when trouble comes. But compassion is not the spiritual force that pushes affliction away, and you won't get out of affliction by turning to others. Athough you might receive encouragement from them, you will only escape hardship when you praise and worship God, obey and confess the Word, stand firmly on God's promises, and pray. That's when you'll see a change.

James 5:14 and 15 says, *"Is any sick among you? Let him call for the elders of the church; and let them pray over him, anointing him with oil in the name of the Lord. And the prayer of faith shall save the sick, and the Lord shall raise him up; and if he have committed sins, they shall be forgiven him."*

Some people say that James is talking about diseases of the mind and soul in these verses, but the Greek word that he uses clearly indicates that he is talking about the diseases that make people physically ill.

Often, when church members get sick, they stay home from church and hope that someone calls them on the telephone. If no one calls, they feel neglected, but they don't do anything themselves to get better. James' instruction explains why those church members don't get healed. When we are physically ill, we should call for the elders of the church so that they can pray over us.

In this situation, it is appropriate for us to call, and it is the church's responsibility to pray. James 5:16 says, *"...The effectual fervent prayer of a righteous man availeth much."*

If I am called to the bedside of a dying man, am I supposed to reassure him that sickness and suffering come from God? Am I supposed to say, "I'll pray for you, brother. I'll pray that you are comforted as you go through your tough time here. Just ride this thing out. God is doing a perfect work in you. God's ways are mysterious sometimes, but all things work together for good in the end, bless your heart"?

No, of course not. James 5:16 says, *"...The effectual fervent prayer of a righteous man availeth much."* We are to pray a prayer of faith, believing as we pray that God will heal and forgive us.

James would not have given the instruction to call for the elders and let them lay hands on you and pray for you if healing had not been a fundamental part of the New Covenant.

Sometimes people say, "We did that in our church one time, and it didn't work. We said, 'Lord, whatever Your will be, let it be done in this life. Heal this one, if it be Thy will.' Nothing happened. No one got healed. In fact, later on, the person we prayed for died. Praying didn't work."

These people did not witness healing because they did not pray as believers who know God's promises. They did not obey James' instruction to pray the *prayer of faith*, which is fervent and effectual.

The man of faith says, "Father, in Jesus' Name, I curse sickness now. Sickness, you leave this body. I release healing now. Be whole!" He doesn't wonder if God might heal someone. He knows that God's desire is to heal, and his prayer is powerful and effective because it is full of faith.

What We *Pray* Can't Override What We *Say*

When I minister to people who have unbelief, I often wish that I could overpower their doubts, but the prayer of faith cannot supersede the confession of unbelief. If you pray for someone who confesses, "I am going to die; I just know it," his confession will nullify your prayer.

However, God wants us to be healed, and we can be assured that when we embrace and confess the truth, the prayer of faith will be answered and our healing will come.

Healing is a part of Jesus' redemptive work. It is an essential part of the New Covenant. Jesus' bruising was for your healing. The injuries that He took in His body purchased healing and health for you, and He wants you to be healed!

CHAPTER FIVE

GOD'S CHARACTER

Religion teaches us that God makes people sick, so when sickness comes, Christians often think, *I don't know if God wants to heal me. Maybe He's trying to teach me a lesson and wants me to have this disease.*

It's not a blessing to be sick, and God never sends sicknesses. While Jesus was on the earth, He never said, "I will bless this person by making him sick. In the long run, it will be a good thing." Sickness is not a good thing!

The only one who brings sickness is the devil. Satan has an opening into our lives because there's a curse in the earth, but Jesus came to redeem us from the curse.

Galatians 1:4 says that Jesus gave Himself for our sins in order to deliver us *"...from this present evil world..."* If He were walking down the hallway of a hospital today, I know that He would have compassion for the sick and injured and would say to everyone who cried out to Him in faith, "Satan has bound you, but I am setting you free. You are delivered from this infirmity."

Because of the truths and promises I have read in the Bible, I am persuaded that believers should not be suffering from sickness and disease.

Perhaps you're thinking, *I don't think of God as a compassionate healer. I can't see Him that way.* Let me encourage you, you will begin to see God as a healer if you examine His character.

The Thorn Issue

Sometimes people misunderstand Scripture, and their confusion about the meaning of a Bible passage becomes a stumbling block to their healing.

Job's story from the Old Testament is a stumbling block for many people because they believe that God made Job sick. However, Job 1:12 says that Satan "put forth his hand." Satan is the one who afflicted Job with sickness, not God.

People also stumble over the New Testament account of Paul's "thorn in the flesh." They say, "Paul had a thorn. He had an incurable eye disease, and his eye disease came from God."

The Greek transcript of the New Testament and the *King James Version* of the Bible do not say that Paul had an eye disease. The *Living Bible,* a Bible paraphrase, says that Paul had an eye disease, but in this case, the *Living Bible* is inaccurate.

Can you imagine Paul preaching and establishing churches with dripping, infected eyes? "I'm sorry," he says, "I'm trying to walk in health, but the Bible hasn't worked for me. Let me lay hands on you and pray for your healing. Maybe God will come through for you."

Paul had a "thorn," which is an Old Testament type for times when one group of people rises up against another group. One group becomes a thorn to the other. Throughout his ministry, Paul dealt with people who opposed him. He was familiar with Old Testament types, so he referred to this persecution, which often endangered his life, as "a thorn in the flesh." Paul was a vigorous man and walked in health. The Bible is clear about that.

The Marvelous Qualities of God

James 1:13-17 says,

Let no man say when he is tempted, I am tempted of God: for God cannot be tempted with evil, neither tempteth he any man: But every man is tempted, when he is drawn away of his own lust, and enticed. Then when lust hath conceived, it bringeth forth sin: and sin, when it is finished, bringeth forth death. Do not err, my beloved brethren. Every good gift and every perfect gift is from above, and cometh down from the Father of lights, with whom is no variableness, neither shadow of turning.

If we want to know what God is like, we don't need to go any further than James 1:13-17, which gives us an accurate description of His character.

Our flesh has evil desires, and we can be drawn away by our own lusts. But God cannot be tempted and drawn away. He is incapable of sin, and every good and perfect gift comes down from Him.

Recently, I heard a minister say on a teaching tape that the Word of God begins to work in our lives when it becomes *exciting* to us, and I believe we need to be excited about James 1. We need to marvel at the qualities of God.

In the Greek, the phrase "cometh down" in verse 17 means, *is constantly coming toward you.* In other words, we have moods and changes, but there is no shadow or variation in God's character. He is always the Father of lights. He is constantly coming toward us with all of His good and perfect gifts.

Sickness is not a good and perfect gift, and He never comes toward us with pain and suffering. God does not make us sick.

God the Nourisher

Genesis 17 provides another look at God's character. This Bible passage describes a conversation between Abram and God. God has promised Abram a son, and for twenty-five years, Abram has been waiting. But the baby has not come, and Abram is disheartened. He is ninety-nine years old, and he believes that he is too old to be a father. He believes that there is no longer any way for God to bring him a miracle. His negative thinking is a hindrance. Before he can receive a son, his thinking needs to change.

When I meet someone who needs a miracle, but doesn't believe that there's a way for God to reach him, I try to change his thinking by showing him God's character. My pattern, or example, is Genesis 17, where God changes Abram's thinking by revealing His character.

In Genesis 17:1, God says, *"...I am the Almighty God; walk before me, and be thou perfect* [blameless, wholehearted, complete].*"*

Certainly, the second part of the verse is important. It is Abram's side of the covenant. However, I want to focus on the first part of the verse, in which God says to Abram, "I am the Almighty God." This is a term for God that means *all-sufficient* or *all-powerful*. It is the aspect of God's character that is interpreted in other parts of the Bible as,"the Supplier, El Shaddai."

We have already discussed the Old Testament image of El Shaddai, in which God is like the mother whose hungry child comes to her to be fed. Like the mother who nurses her hungry child, God nourishes us.

In Genesis 17, God says to Abram, "Come to Me, and I will nourish you with abundance. I will give you health and prosperity. Whatever you need, I will nourish you with that thing if you will come to Me."

People often think, *God is sitting in Heaven with a divine sledgehammer, and if I mess up, He will punish me. If I don't stay on the straight and narrow, He will slap me with something like a business crisis, conflicts in my relationships, or disease.*

When they see Genesis 17, they say, "Well, that was Abraham. He was special. That was in the Old Testament."

However, the Bible says that those who place their faith in Jesus Christ are the sons of Abraham. Galatians 3:9 says that we are blessed and favored by God and are partners in fellowship with Abraham. And Galatians 3:29 says that we are Abraham's seed. When we trust Jesus, we are following after Abraham and have the same promises and blessings that Abraham had. God, who is the Supplier, gives us the same prosperity and abundance that He gave to Abraham.

God as Our Shield and Exceeding Great Reward

Genesis 15:1 provides another description of God's character.

The previous chapter, Genesis 14, talks about the first war in Scripture. The kings of Sodom and Gomorrah are defeated by an alliance of Sumerian kings, and Lot is captured. Abram and his *trained* servants pursue the Sumerian army. By night, they attack and rout the army, rescue Lot, and retrieve all of Sodom and Gomorrah's stolen goods. At the end of Genesis 14, Abram pays his tithe to Melchizedek, king of Salem, who is identified as the priest of God.

Genesis 15:1 says, *"After these things the word of the Lord came unto Abram in a vision, saying, 'Fear not, Abram: I am thy shield, and thy exceeding great reward.'"*

Once again, God reveals His character to Abraham.

God is our shield, or protector. He is not the one who brings trouble; He is the One who strengthens and protects us when the day of trouble comes. He is not the one who brings sickness, but if sickness attacks us, He protects us from sickness' assault.

God is also our "exceeding great reward." The original Hebrew text can also be translated, "rapid, speedy supply of increase or money."

Most of us, as children, encountered bullies who teased and embarrassed us. They stole our lunch money, picked fights with us, or knocked us off of our bikes. We make the mistake of believing that God is a bully too. However, the bully who pesters and overpowers us is not imitating the Father. He is manifesting the character of the enemy.

God has a giving character. He gives peace in the day of trouble and victory in the day of war. He gives protection and financial supply, and He does not try to take anything away.

Forty-nine times in the Old Testament, God says that He is God our Supplier, El Shaddai.

He never says, "I am the God who makes you sick." Sixty-two times in the Old Testament, He reveals Himself as Jehovah Rapha, the Lord Your Healer, the God who heals, the One who heals your diseases. And we saw that in Hebrew, Jehovah Rapha means, *the one who stitches you up and makes you whole.*

When I attend funerals of young people, I often hear comments like this: "The Lord took him away."

When I talk to parents who have lost babies, they occasionally say, "God took my baby home because He needs another angel in Heaven."

These comments grieve me because I know that God is not a taker. The thief is the one who comes to steal, kill, and destroy.

It is an unfortunate tragedy when people die prematurely, but we must not think that God took them or that He needed them in heaven. God wants us to recover from our illnesses and to complete our lives on earth.

God Our Rewarder

Hebrews 11:6 says that God is a *rewarder* of those who diligently seek Him. The Greek word for rewarder means, *to give out* or *to recompense*. It paints the picture of an employer who gives paychecks to his employees.

People sometimes say, "God gave me this blessing, but I haven't been living right, and now He is trying to take it away."

Certainly, if you slip into sin, your wrong living may cause you to lose something that you value. However, God does not take it away. It is not in His nature to take. His nature is to give. In fact, James 1:5 says, "*If any of you lack wisdom, let him ask of God, that giveth to all men liberally, and upbraideth not, and it shall be given him.*"

God gives liberally, which means that He gives freely and bountifully. He is always ready to help people who are in trouble.

Matthew 9 and Mark 5 tell the story of a woman who was healed of "an issue of blood."

If we understand the way this woman came to Jesus, we will also begin to understand the way our healing comes.

For twelve years, this woman had suffered from an illness that caused her to bleed; and even though she had gone to many doctors, she had not improved. Instead, she had spent all of her money and had grown steadily worse.

One day, this woman heard about Jesus. She began to say to herself, *If I can only touch His garment, I shall be restored to health.*

Religious laws prohibited her from leaving her home, but she went to Jesus anyway. Religious law required that she confess her unworthiness by saying, "Unclean! Unclean!" as she walked along, but she confessed Jesus instead.

She kept saying to herself, *If I can only touch His garment, I shall be restored to health.*

A huge crowd of people was packed together, thronging Jesus. Even though the woman was physically weak, she worked her way through the crowd, came up behind Jesus, touched the hem of His garment, and was healed.

Immediately, Jesus turned to His disciples and said, "Who touched Me?"

That's a funny thing for a man to ask when He is being thronged, but Jesus felt healing power flow out of Him, and He was actually asking, "Who touched Me with such faith that healing was pulled from Me?"

The woman with the issue of blood heard Jesus' question and fell on her knees, trembling. She told Jesus everything.

Jesus must have been thinking, *Why are you trembling? My goodness, I commend you! In this doubting, wavering, fearful generation, I marvel at your faith.*

When Jesus responded to this woman, He didn't say, "I am like a bolt of lightning. I am such a powerful carrier of healing power that anyone who touches Me will be healed." And He didn't say, "My faith has healed you." Instead, He said, "*Your* faith has healed you." This woman put her faith into action, and she was healed by her faith.

God Our Loving Father

I am trying to "pound" the truth of God's goodness into your heart so that you will never again respond to Satan's destructive work by saying, "God must have done this to me."

Matthew 7:11 says, *"If ye then, being evil* [carnal, or natural], *know how to give good gifts unto your children, how much more shall your Father which is in heaven give good things to them that ask him?"*

Matthew 7:11 reveals God's character by comparing Him to an earthly father. We have the desire to give good gifts to our children, even though we are imperfect and natural. But God, who is our Heavenly Father, has an even greater desire to bless us. He wants to give us good gifts, and He wants us to enjoy the gifts that He gives.

My father had seven sons. While I was growing up, there were times that he worked three different jobs so that he could buy enough food and clothing for all of us. When I was a little boy, he even built a house all by himself. He didn't know how to build a house in the beginning, but he learned as he went along. He worked on that house for five years because he loved his sons and wanted us to have a nice home. My dad is a believer today, but in those days, he was not. He was a natural, unredeemed man, but he still wanted to give good gifts to his sons.

God is a loving Father, and He is able to love us perfectly. He has perfect gifts and wants to give those perfect gifts to us. It is God's character to give us things. *It is not His character to take things away.*

In fact, Romans 8:32 (NKJV) says, *"He who did not spare His own Son, but delivered Him up for us all, how shall He not with Him also freely give us all things?"*

In this verse, the word "freely" means, *to show favor or kindness* or *to be gracious toward someone.* God has already given us Jesus. Now He wants to be gracious toward us and give us all of His other good things too.

We see, then, that God is a giver. He is El Shaddai, our nourisher, according to Genesis 17:1. He is our protector and great reward. He is our Father, according to Matthew 7:11, and He loves us so much that He gave us His son.

God is able to make every earthly blessing come to us in abundance, and He is such a generous and loving Father that He looks for ways to give us everything. This is His character.

CHAPTER SIX

STEPPING OVER INTO YOUR
REALM OF AUTHORITY

If a robber was to break into our home, we wouldn't say, "This must be God's will for me." We would say, "I am being attacked." We'd call 9-1-1, and while we were waiting for the police to arrive, we'd take steps to protect ourselves.

Sickness and disease are enemies too. Like all other unlawful forces, they threaten our peace and security. And if they attack us, we need to fight back with boldness and authority.

Sometimes, I meet people who say, "I'm sick, and I need to be healed, so I am waiting on the Lord. I know that the time will come when I will step out and get healed."

My response to them is, "Why are you waiting? Be bold. Step into your realm of authority, and get healed today!"

God on the Inside of Us

Genesis 1:26 says that we are made in the image of God. Just as our sons and daughters are made of our fiber and resemble us, we as God's children are made of God's fiber and resemble Him. Psalm 82:6 says, *"...Ye are gods; and all of you are children of the most High,"* and Jesus teaches the same principle in John 10.

In John 10:27, Jesus says, *"My sheep hear my voice, and I know them, and they follow me."*

Many voices try to get our attention, but it should comfort us to know that we can know the voice of God and can be led by Him.

Verses 28 and 29 say, *"And I give unto them eternal life; and they shall never perish, neither shall any man pluck them out of my hand. My Father, which gave them to me, IS GREATER THAN ALL; and no man is able to pluck them out of my Father's hand."*

The word "greater" comes from the Greek root word "megas," and it means, *biggest, greatest.* It is the basis for English expressions like megamall and megastar. Jesus is saying, "My Father is mega. He is bigger and greater than them all—greater than any problem you face."

In John 10:30, Jesus says, "I and My Father are One."

Of course, this statement infuriated some of the Jewish people who were listening to Jesus. He claimed to be one with God, and they protested, "Sacrilege!" They picked up rocks so that they could stone Him.

Jesus answered them perfectly: *"...Many good works have I shewed you from my Father; for which of those works do ye stone me?"* (v. 32).

The Jews answered Him, "...*For a good work we stone thee not; but for blasphemy; and because that thou, being a man, makest thyself God*" (v. 33).

Jesus responded, "*Is it not written in your law, I said, Ye are gods?*" (v. 34). He was referring to Psalm 82:6.

Throughout the New Testament, the Greek word used for God is the word "theos," which means, *Supreme Being* or *Godhead*. "Theos" is also used in John 10:34. In other words, Jesus asked the Jewish people who accused Him of blasphemy, "Doesn't it say in your Law that you are gods?"

Certainly, we are not part of the Godhead, and if we come from certain religious backgrounds, the very suggestion that we are gods makes us uneasy. Jesus is not saying that we are God. He is saying that we are created in God's likeness.

Made to Exercise Dominion on Earth

Second Corinthians 4:4 says that Satan is the god of this world. He has the legal right to manipulate circumstances and unwitting people, because he has authority.

How did Satan get his authority? He got it from Adam. When Satan came into the Garden, Adam was the god of this earth, and when Adam sinned, he gave Satan his authority.

Adam was not God, I am not God, and you are not God. However, we are made in the likeness of God, and God created us so that we could be His representatives.

"Well," you say, "Satan got all the authority. I have no authority."

Jesus, as part of His redemptive work, bought back your authority. Jesus defeated the devil, and as a child of God, you have dominion over the work of the enemy.

This dominion applies to any area of your life, from business and family relationships to sickness and disease.

Often, I talk to people who are comfortable with the idea that God has given dominion to ministers. "That's right, Pastor," they say, "God has equipped you to deal with wickedness in high places [Eph. 6:12] and to pray for people so that they can be healed. You have His anointing and authority."

These people would never think of casting out a devil or laying hands on the sick themselves. Instead, they call the church so that someone on the pastoral staff can do that for them. They have no revelation about their own dominion.

If you are a born-again believer, you have authority. You rule over everything in Satan's kingdom, and it is written in the Word that you were made to be like God. You have authority over any darkness that tries to cover your life, including sickness and disease.

Romans 5:17 says, *"For if by one man's offense death reigned by one; much more they which receive abundance of grace and of the gift of righteousness shall reign in life by one, Jesus Christ."*

The Greek word "basileuo" is used two times in Romans 5:17. It means, *to reign, to rule,* or *to exercise kingly power.*

According to Romans 5:17, death reigned as king because of Adam's offense, but life reigns as king because of Jesus Christ.

Most religious people agree that sin rules in people's lives because of Adam's disobedience. "Yes, Pastor, sin is king," they say.

In order to understand what the Bible is telling us, however, we need to read beyond the first part of the verse, which says, *"For if by one man's offense death reigned by one..."* The rest of that verse says, *"...much more they which receive abundance of grace and of the gift of righteousness shall reign in life by one, Jesus Christ."*

In other words, it says, "Because you have received an abundance of grace (which is salvation) and the gift of righteousness, *you* shall reign as a king. You shall have kingly power in this life, and you shall rule as a king throughout eternity."

Pastors preach about dominion, but I don't think most of us have the revelation we could possess concerning our authority. If Christians understood their authority, they would look at sickness and say, "You must leave." They would refuse to allow fear into their lives. They would say to anxiety, "I have dominion. I rule in this situation and you don't, so I am commanding you to go." They would say to trouble, "I have authority over you."

Instead, Christians often pray, "I am overwhelmed by trouble. Jesus, come soon."

We need to get it inside our spirits that we have authority. We need to get to the point of realizing that we rule over sickness and that it does not rule over us.

We need to get this revelation: "I'm reigning in this life because of Jesus Christ. I am ruling on this earth by Him."

Most of us need to get out of our natural minds so that we can begin to listen to our hearts and to the things that the Word says to us. Our minds say, "Yes, *but* I know of a Christian who died. Yes, *but* I know of trouble that came. Yes, *but* I know that I have pain. Yes, *but* I don't feel strong enough to rise up from sickness. Yes, *but* I feel inadequate. Yes, *but* I am worried and skeptical. Yes, *but*…"

It is important for us to realize that we cannot allow these things to reign over us. We need to walk in the truth of Romans 5:17. If we have received the abundance of grace, which is salvation, and if we have received the free gift of righteousness, then we reign in life by the One, Jesus Christ.

Jesus is remarkable. He went into hell, defeated Satan, rose from the dead, sat down at the right hand of God, and continues to reign after two thousand years. Obviously, if we are depending on our own strength, we cannot be like Him. But, if we are born again, His very nature is in us, and we rule on earth by Him.

The principles of ruling and reigning work in any area of life, and we need to instill these truths in our children. Every morning, before they leave for school, we need to tell them, "You're a child of the King, and because of Him, you rule and reign over every test you take and every challenge you face. You rule over every problem that comes across your path today, including sickness and disease. Because of Jesus, you're a priest. You rule over the work of the devil because Jesus made you a king."

His Life in Us

In John 6:63, Jesus says, *"It is the Spirit that quickeneth; the flesh profiteth nothing; the words that I speak unto you, they are spirit, and they are life."*

Most of us have gotten the revelation that our flesh does not profit us and that we are not going to find truth and life by listening to it.

However, Jesus says that His words give us truth and life. In fact, He says that His words are zoë life, which is a heavenly, abundant, eternal, life-giving, God-kind of life. When we are born again, His zoë life begins to live on the inside of us.

When sickness and disease come, we need to use God's life-giving, eternal, zoë life to look boldly at sickness and say, "I'm going to attack you. Get off of my family member. Get off of my neighbor. Get off of me."

John G. Lake, the great evangelist, meditated on the Word. According to a book that was written by his son-in-law, Lake had a true revelation of John 6:63. He realized that since the words of Jesus were spirit and life, and since Jesus was in him, then his words could be spirit and life too.

Lake believed that when he spoke a word to sickness, sickness had to listen to him because Jesus was speaking through him. He believed that his words became spirit and life because Jesus' words were spirit and life.

John G. Lake witnessed many healing miracles in his ministry. For example, he lived in Africa for several years, and he encountered plagues for which there was no medical cure. These plagues were so deadly that people were afraid to touch them.

However, Lake had a revelation about the power of Jesus' words. He often said the life of God lived on the inside of him, and because he meditated on the Word, then he could take authority over plagues. He believed that when plagues came in contact with him, they had to die because his words were spirit and life.

Sure enough, doctors would put tissue samples under the microscope after he had spoken to the plague and would verify that the plague cells in the sample had died.

He was also able to lay his hands on any man or woman and determine the exact nature of that person's disease. Time after time, Lake's diagnoses were proven to be correct.

I think one of Lake's greatest achievements was starting the healing rooms in Washington. Most of the people who worked with Lake have gone on to be with the Lord, and the healing rooms were closed for a while. They were reopened recently, and workers there are getting the same results that Lake and his associates did.

Christian workers meditated on the Word until it became spirit and life to them, and then they ministered healing to the sick. The workers told those they ministered to that their words were spirit and life, and the illness had to die because of the words they spoke.

When the sick person left the healing room, he was healed.

You can also speak words that are spirit and life. Begin by getting into the Word of God. Meditate on the Word and confess it until the words that are in the Bible become real to you and begin to come out of your heart. After that, take the words that come out of your heart and speak them to various sicknesses. For example, say,

"Cancer, you have to leave. Diabetes, you have to go. Back, you are healed, in Jesus' Name."

John 6:63 says, *"It is the spirit that quickeneth . . . "* The Spirit of God makes alive. When you speak the Word of God into a situation, your words become spirit and life. They come from the Eternal Nature, and when you speak them, they produce healing and victory.

Empowered Through Fellowship

I know people who have the Greater One in them, but when they speak the Word, nothing happens. They are well equipped, yet they get no results. Power comes as a result of fellowship with God, and they have gotten out of fellowship with Him, so their power is dormant.

If you want to speak words of life, you have to stay in fellowship with God.

Frequently, people get out of fellowship with Him because of the thoughts that fill their minds.

For example, they think, *I hate So-and-so,* and they are pulled out of fellowship. Or they meditate on hurtful things that were done to them, and they are pulled out of fellowship. God is not mad at them, but wrong thinking has disconnected them from Him.

The Word is clear about how much God wants to bless us and answer our prayers, but we can stop His movement in our lives. When our prayers aren't answered, we want to blame God. But God is always moving, and if we are powerless, we are the ones who have broken the flow.

Colossians 2:13 and 14 says, *"And you, being dead in your sins and the uncircumcision of your flesh, hath he quickened* [made alive] *together with him, having forgiven you all trespass-*

es; Blotting out the handwriting of ordinances that was against us, which was contrary to us, and took it out of the way, nailing it to his cross."

In other words, because we came from the seed of Adam, we were sinners. Laws were written against us, and we were on our way to hell, but Jesus blotted out the handwriting of the law and restored our relationship with God through the Cross. God paid a very dear price, His Son, for us to fellowship with Him freely.

When we allow the things and cares of this world to fill our minds, we are out of fellowship with God, and we obstruct the flow of His power in our lives. When that happens simply say, "God, please forgive me," make an adjustment in your thinking, and get back in fellowship, and into a place of empowerment.

Some Spoiled, Some Empowered

Colossians 2:15 says, *"And having spoiled principalities and powers, he made a shew of them openly. . ."*

The word "principality" comes from the Greek word "arch," which means, *primary power* or *chief.* An archangel is an angel at the highest level of authority, either in God's kingdom or in the demonic realm.

Colossians 2:15 refers to the leaders of Satan's realm and says that Jesus spoiled them. In other words, they were armed, but Jesus disarmed them. They had a kingdom, but Jesus plundered it.

According to Luke 10:19, Jesus gave us power: *"Behold, I give unto you power to tread on serpents and scorpions, and OVER ALL THE POWER OF THE ENEMY: and nothing shall by any means hurt you."*

Certainly, the enemy, Satan, has supernatural power, but we have been authorized by Jesus to trample on it. In Luke 10:19, He tells us that He gave us authority over *all* the power of the evil one. If Satan continues to exercise authority on this earth, it is because we allow him to.

We see that we are made of God's fiber and in His image. We were created to be His representatives on earth and to rule on His behalf. Adam gave his authority to Satan, but Jesus returned it to us. When we are in fellowship with Him, our very words contain "spirit and life" and enable us to trample on Satan's power and authority.

When we are in fellowship with God, we don't have to work hard to get heavenly power. Heavenly power flows out of our relationship with Him. We simply need to learn how to step over into our God-given authority.

CHAPTER SEVEN

THE GODHEAD DWELLS IN YOU

When believers get sick, they often think that they have done something wrong and are sick because God is teaching them a lesson. They think that if they resist the illness, they are resisting Him.

However, there is no sickness in Heaven, and God does not send sickness to earth. If He needs to correct us, He uses the convicting power of His Word and His Holy Spirit, but sickness is not one of His teaching tools.

Sickness is the work of the enemy, and if sickness comes, God wants us to *bind it up.*

Certainly, without the help of Jesus, we do not have the authority to bind sickness and disease.

Jesus says in Matthew 16:19, *"And I will give unto thee the keys of the kingdom of heaven: and whatsoever thou shalt bind on earth shall be bound in heaven: and whatsoever thou shalt loose on earth shall be loosed in heaven."*

"Keys" represent authority. And when Jesus turns to His disciples and says, "I am giving you the keys," He is giving them the power to operate in His kingdom.

It's as if I own a home, and one day I give you a key. "Use my home whenever you need to," I say. "You are welcome to come in at any time." Suddenly, you are not an outsider anymore. By giving you the key, I have authorized you to come into my house and use everything I own.

You wouldn't have to ask yourself, "Do I have the right to go into this house?" By giving you a key and inviting you to use it, I have authorized you to unlock the door and make yourself at home.

Jesus is inviting us to operate in God's Kingdom, and He is giving us the keys. We don't have to ask ourselves, "Do I have the right to bind and loose?" In Matthew 16:19, Jesus tells us that we do.

Obedience Produces the Power to Bind and Loose

Of course, we can't live in disobedience and have supernatural authority at the same time. If we are disobeying the Word, we will say, "I bind and loose in Jesus' Name" without accomplishing anything.

On the other hand, we don't have to live perfectly in order to have Jesus' authority. We simply need to do our best to live righteously.

We need to say, "I'm going to seek first the Kingdom of God, and I am going to do everything I can to live right for God." If you are living for God, you have the right to use Jesus' authority over anything the devil brings into your life.

Miracles Outside the Church Walls

Recently, a group of Christians who attend our Sunday night services ministered in another country. They were amazed by the miracles they witnessed. When they got back, they said, "Ears opened, blind people received sight. Things happened that we don't see at home."

They were like the Seventy who returned to Jesus in Luke 10:17. They came back with joy, amazed that even the devils were subject to them in Jesus' Name.

Often, people in foreign countries are like sponges. When we witness to them, they soak up the truth that we share. When we say, "Jesus heals," they have no skepticism. They simply say, "Come on, then. Get me healed."

It should be just as easy for Christians to be healed as it is for people from other religious backgrounds, but Christians are not always willing to believe that God wants to heal them. They say, "Jesus doesn't heal. I know, because my aunt served God for years, but she was in a wheelchair, and she was never healed."

Our churches are hindered by unbelief.

Often, Christians think that people can't be healed until they are saved. They say to the unbeliever, "Get everything in your life straightened out, and God will heal you. Receive Jesus as your Savior, and He will give you health."

However, the Bible does not say that salvation is a prerequisite for healing. In fact, God often uses healing as His "drawing card." He knows that people are more likely to receive Jesus Christ if He heals them, so He restores them on credit, so to speak, so that after they are healed, they will get saved. Certainly, some people use their credit for a long time, but God is merciful.

God wants His Church to be powerful, but if we want to see healing miracles, we usually have to leave the four walls of the church.

Take healing to the unbelievers. Allow God's miraculous healing power to flow among them. Their testimonies will persuade church members that God is their Healer, and healing will come back into the Church.

Get the Strife Out!

Salvation includes healing, and God wants every believer to be healthy and vigorous. However, He cannot bring healing if your heart is full of contempt. We block His healing power when our lives are filled with strife.

We say, "So-and-so didn't speak to me after church last Sunday. She didn't invite me out to lunch. A whole week went by, and she didn't even call me on the telephone. What kind of friend is that?"

And then we share our offense with everyone we know.

Or we say, "I don't think the pastor paid enough attention to me at a meeting last week, and he didn't shake my hand after church. My feelings are hurt."

And then we criticize the pastor when we are with our Christian friends.

We enter the realm of strife and cling to our offense. We cry out to Jesus, "We need healing." And He is saying, "Strife is keeping you from receiving your healing."

There is no anointing, and there is no flow of the Spirit where there is strife.

If we continue to hold on to strife, our money begins to dwindle, our bodies get sick, and we don't have any peace.

"I don't understand why this isn't working," we say, and we start blaming God.

Perhaps you have noticed that when you were in the world, you weren't in strife with your friends all the time. If they didn't speak to you one day, you weren't offended, and you didn't keep track of how often they complimented you, invited you out to lunch, or called you on the telephone. But now, you have a little scorecard in your head, and when people don't live up to your expectations, you complain.

When Jesus says in Luke 10:18, ". . . I beheld Satan as lightning fall from heaven." He identifies our problem. Satan isn't in Heaven anymore. He is on earth, deceiving people and stirring up strife.

He sends out whiny little weasel demons that sit on our shoulders and whisper in our ears. When we listen to them, we become whiners, too. Most people don't want to spend time with a whiner.

We want to see God's glory, and we want to have healing, but His glory and healing do not come when our lives are filled with discord and contention. God loves you, and He still lives in you, but He can't work through you when your life is filled with strife.

In Matthew 18:7, Jesus says that offenses will come. As long as we are on earth, we will have opportunities to get our feelings hurt.

On a typical Sunday morning, there is always someone in the service who doesn't like what I say from the Word.

Every Sunday morning, I have opportunities to become insulted and upset. I've learned to fear God, but to have no fear of man. If someone doesn't like the sermon, I've learned to say, "That doesn't bother me."

The devil loves it when Christians get offended because he knows that strife blocks the power of God. However, God has given us the authority to resist *all* the enemy's power, including the power of strife.

Binding and Loosing

Matthew 16:19 says, *"...whatsoever thou shalt bind on earth SHALL BE BOUND in heaven: and whatsoever thou shalt loose on earth SHALL BE LOOSED in heaven."* The phrases "shall be bound" and "shall be loosed" were written in the Greek as *future-perfect passive participles,* which, in effect, describe the action as having already happened. In other words, whatsoever we bind on earth *shall have already been bound* in Heaven.

Heaven has already bound and loosed, and Jesus authorizes us to bind and loose on earth what has already been bound and loosed in Heaven.

Jesus is saying, "I'm giving you the keys, so you can be sure that your binding and loosing will work. Just be sure to bind and loose the same things that Heaven has already bound and loosed." The Book of Acts is filled with stories of followers who learned how to bind and loose and saw miraculous results.

Complete in Christ

Certainly, as believers, we want to bind sickness, loose healing, take authority over the devil, get rid of sickness in our families, and minister healing to other people. Colossians 2 tells us how to position ourselves to do so. Colossians 2:6 says, *"As you have therefore received Christ Jesus the Lord, so walk ye in him."*

If we are "in Him," we are locked in. Colossians 2:7-10 says,

> *Rooted and built up in him, and stablished in the faith, as ye have been taught, abounding therein with thanksgiving. Beware lest any man spoil you through philosophy and vain deceit, after the tradition of men, after the rudiments of the world, and not after Christ. For in him dwelleth all the fullness of the Godhead bodily. AND YE ARE COMPLETE IN HIM, which is the head of all principality and power.*

All of the Godhead is locked up in the body of Jesus Christ, who is the full expression of Father, Son, and Holy Ghost. There is a lot of power locked up in Jesus, and He says, "I give that power to you." His power makes us complete.

However, the last phrase of Colossians 2:7-10 is the central point of the passage. It says, *"...which is the head of all principality and power."*

Principality, as we have already learned, means "primary power," "chief," or "highest-ranking power." When we talk about the angelic host, it means "archangel," or "angel in charge." Jesus is greater than every other spiritual authority, whether in Heaven or hell. The angelic host is huge, but His power surpasses the power of any angelic force, whether it is heavenly or demonic, and we have access to His power.

Jesus' power is stronger than the power of cancer, and when we speak to cancer in His Name, cancer must listen to us. His power is greater than paralysis or heart disease.

His power is stronger than Satan's power, and when we come up against the devil, the devil has to obey us in Jesus' Name.

Sometimes, we are very casual about the Name of Jesus. We use it almost as loosely as we would use a lucky charm or a rabbit's foot.

We need to have a revelation of the power behind Jesus' Name. Philippians 2:10 says that it is the name above every name. At the Name of Jesus, *every* knee shall bow, whether that knee is in Heaven, on earth, or in hell; and He gave us the right to use His Name.

When evil challenges us, we can say, "No, no. I have a revelation about the power of the Name of Jesus. Evil, you cannot stay. Satan, you have to go."

Colossians 1:25 says, "*Whereof I am made a minister according to the dispensation* [or mystery] *of God which is given to me for you, to fulfil the word of God.*"

This verse defines Paul's ministry. The Church Age was a mystery to the generations who lived under the Old Covenant. It was not even revealed to Daniel or Isaiah. Paul, through divine revelation, explained the mystery.

Colossians 1:26 and 27 says, "*Even the mystery which hath been hid from ages and from generations, but now*

is made manifest to his saints: To whom God would make
known what is the riches of the glory of this mystery among the
Gentiles; which is Christ in you, the hope of glory."

Christ in us—this is the mystery that was revealed
to the New Testament Church by Paul. We hear the
phrase so often that it loses its significance, but it needs
to be real to us. Christ, the Messiah, *lives* in us. All of God
is in Christ, and when we are born again, all of Christ
dwells in us. *Christ in us*, the hope of glory, will take care
of the problems we face.

Christ is in you. The Father, the Creator, actually
dwells in you!

If you can get a revelation that the One who said,
"Let there be light" and caused the universe to be formed
is living on the inside of you, you won't worry about
things anymore.

Bold for God

I know a lot of people who used to live boldly for
the devil. They drank, cursed, acted mean, and served
Satan without any shyness. Now that they have come to
God, they're restrained. "I know I should be witnessing
at work, but I'm just struggling," they say. "If the right
door opens, maybe. I don't know. I need some boldness,
Lord."

After we become believers, we sometimes hide
Jesus, but we need to be as bold for Jesus as we used to
be for the devil when we were living for him. When we
wake up in the morning, we need to say, "Christ is in me,
and Christ in me is supposed to shine forth and be seen.

I am going to look for opportunities to tell people that He is in me today."

Early in my Christian walk, I worked at a warehouse where I unloaded trucks. It was a tough job because many of the people I spent my day with used drugs, swore, and told dirty jokes.

Every morning, I read my Bible and prayed before I went to work. After a while, I began to think, *Why am I doing this every morning? If I'm not going to use my Christianity at work, what good does reading the Bible do? I'm going to start looking for opportunities to share the truth from the Bible at work.*

Before long, an unsaved woman who worked on the docks came up to me one morning and said, "My doctor just told me that I have breast cancer, and I want you and your Christian friends to lay hands on me and pray."

She actually used the expression, *"lay hands on me."*

At lunchtime, two other guys and I went outside for lunch and said to the woman, "We're going to pray for you. Lift up your hands to the Lord. We'll put our hands on your hands, and then we will pray."

We prayed for her, and when she went back to the doctor, he took an X-ray and told her, "Your cancer has disappeared. It's gone."

All of a sudden, my Christian friends and I were known as "the people who could get rid of cancer." We didn't mind. Our coworker's healing had opened doors for us with other people in the company.

Jesus Christ had the keys to the Kingdom, but He gave those keys to you, along with His authority. If you are a believer, you are in Christ, and He is living in you, which means that all of the power of the Godhead resides inside of you. Jesus goes to church with you, but He also goes to work with you. When you are bold enough to let Him work through you, His power starts flowing out of you. Healing begins to manifest in the lives of the people who work and live around you, and miracles begin to occur.

CHAPTER EIGHT

AUTHORITY AND KEYS—
THE POWER OF BEING IN CHRIST

Sometimes I lose my keys. One day, for example, I laid them down in the shopping cart while I paid for groceries, and then I forgot to pick them up. Fortunately, the cashier put them in a safe place. Later, when I went back to the grocery store to look for them, they were still there.

However, let's say that I leave my keys on the church pew while I'm preaching. Someone sees them, picks them up, and says to you, "Guess what? Here are the keys to Pastor Mike's house. I found them on the front row of the church. Take these keys and go stay over there."

Although you have the keys, you don't have them legally, and you are not empowered to unlock my front door and stay in my house.

But the situation is very different if I come up to you and say, "Here are the keys to my house. You can have them. I'm going away for awhile, and while I am gone, you have my permission to stay in my house. Go ahead. Make yourself at home." You have the right and authority to stay at my house because I *gave* authority to you.

This is what Jesus did. Sickness and poverty do not have authority over us. We have authority over them because Jesus gave us the keys.

Jesus Gave Us That Job

Although it may be hard for you to believe, Jesus' hands are tied. He is sovereign. He has supreme power, but He can not go back on His Word.

In Matthew 16:19, Jesus says to His disciples, *"...I will give unto thee the keys of the kingdom of heaven: and whatsoever thou shalt bind on earth shall be bound in heaven: and whatsoever thou shalt loose on earth shall be loosed in heaven."* When Jesus gave us the keys, He gave *us* dominion on the earth. He can not work on earth unless we allow Him to work through us.

To illustrate this point, let's say that one day you find yourself in a critical situation. You've been saying that God teaches people lessons by making them sick, and Satan is having a field day. You're sick nearly every day.

You cry out to Jesus, "Bind up Satan. Tell him to stop putting these sicknesses on me." And Jesus responds, "I gave you the keys. I gave you the authority to bind sickness and I can't take that authority back. I can't go against My Word. Binding Satan is your job, so use your authority. It's not hard. I am living in you, so he's not bigger or stronger than you. You have the power to whip him, so whip him!"

We make it harder than it needs to be, simply because of unbelief. Too often our focus is on our abilities, and not on the abilities of Christ in us.

God is powerful, but He can't do anything on this earth unless we say it, believe it, and stand on it, because Jesus gave us the keys!

For example, God wants the Gospel to be preached throughout the world, and He wants every person on earth to be saved, but He can't get people saved unless He has an obedient, willing person down here on earth. Matthew 28:19 tells us to go and teach all the nations. Jesus doesn't do the preaching, and He doesn't send angels to preach. In this dispensation, He has given the job of preaching the Gospel to *us*.

If we don't preach the Gospel, the Gospel won't be preached.

When trouble comes, we also have the job of standing in faith on God's Word so that healing and deliverance can come. We go into our place of prayer with our Bibles and find our answer. We write down every Scripture that God quickens to our spirit, and when the devil tries to tell us that we will never be healed, we say, "Shut up, devil. I am not listening to you. I am listening to the Word. I bind you in Jesus' Name." And then we start confessing the Bible verses that God's Spirit has illuminated for us.

However, if we don't do our job, healing won't come.

Signs Should Follow the Believer

We shouldn't have to work hard to convince people of the truth, but when they hear about binding and loosing, they often say, "No, that's false doctrine. That's 'name-it-and-claim-it' stuff."

Through the years, I have often thought, *How can I do a better job of presenting these Bible principles? Which Bible verses can I use to prove to others that the things I am saying to them are true?*

I have learned to go to Mark 16. Mark 16:15 and 16 says, *"And he [Jesus] said unto them, Go ye into all the world, and preach the gospel to every creature. He that believeth and is baptized shall be saved; but he that believeth not shall be damned."*

Everyone would probably agree that preaching the Gospel is Jesus' instruction to all believers. It didn't stop with Peter or Paul. It's still the Church's job.

Every believer would probably also agree that every human being, whether he was born while Jesus was alive or is living now, has an opportunity to be saved. Salvation didn't end with the disciples; it is also for today.

In the next two verses, Mark 16:17 and 18, Jesus says, *"And these signs shall follow them that believe; In my name shall they cast out devils; they shall speak with new tongues; They shall take up serpents; and if they drink any deadly thing, it shall not hurt them; they shall lay hands on the sick, and they shall recover."*

If Mark 16:15 and 16 is for everyone, then Mark 16:17 and 18 is for everyone too. Even if we don't like the last two verses, we can't simply throw them out. In order to have a valid belief system, we have to accept Mark 16:17 and 18 too.

If we are called to preach the Gospel, we're also called to demonstrate the signs. That's part of our job.

Signs are supposed to follow us, and distinguish us from others (Mark 16:17).

If we obey Jesus' entire instruction, we will see the revival that we often talk about.

Five Signs

One of the signs that is supposed to walk alongside believers and distinguish us from everyone else is this: *We cast out devils.* It's part of our job. It's one of the things that Jesus has given us authority to do.

Many Christians say that casting out devils is not for today, but I have cast out devils and have seen them leave, and I was doing this before I became a pastor. I know that casting out devils is a valid principle for twenty-first century Christianity.

Another sign that should follow us is *speaking with new tongues.* Some people say, "When Jesus says that we will talk with new tongues, He means that after we are born again, we'll have a different point of view and will start talking differently." Certainly, the born-again experience changes our perception of things, but new tongues are unknown languages that begin to flow out of us. One of the signs that should follow all believers is the gift of speaking in tongues.

A third sign that should follow us is that we *"take up serpents."*

Perhaps you don't mind snakes, but I hate them more than anything else. I certainly don't want to pick up a snake, and this is not what Jesus is telling us to do. He is referring to situations like Paul's experience in Acts 28.

Paul is a prisoner. The Roman government is transporting him by boat from Jerusalem to Rome. The boat encounters a terrible storm and is destroyed, but no one aboard the ship dies. Everyone swims to the island of Malta, where they make a camp and build a fire on the shore.

Paul gathers a bundle of sticks, and there is a poisonous snake hiding inside the bundle. While Paul is putting the sticks on the fire, the snake crawls out of them because of the heat and bites Paul on the arm.

The Maltese people, who are helping him, assume that he is a criminal who is receiving justice from their gods, even though he survived the storm. They wait for Paul to swell up or drop dead, but nothing harmful ever happens to him. After a while, they are so amazed that they begin to call him a god.

Paul says, "I am not a god. I am just as natural and human as you are." But Paul knows that Jesus has given him authority over snakes, so when a poisonous snake crawls out of hiding and bites him, he exercises his authority. We have this same authority!

A fourth sign that should follow believers is this: *If we eat or drink anything deadly, it will not hurt us.* More often than we'd like to think, we eat deadly things in restaurants, or out of our refrigerators at home. So we handle the threat of spoiled food by standing on the Word on a daily basis and saying, "Nothing I eat and nothing I touch can hurt me." We have authority over all of these things.

Our fifth sign as believers is this: *We lay hands on the sick, and they will recover.* Please remember that Jesus is saying this to all who *believe.* If you don't believe, it won't work for you, and that's why so many Christians don't see healings. They are hindered by unbelief. However, Jesus gives the instruction to lay hands on the sick to the same group of people He gives the instruction to preach the Gospel. It's part of what all believers are equipped and commanded to do.

In Mark 16:18, the word "recover" means, *to be well, to be made well, to be healed.*

James 5 tells us that if we are sick, we can call the elders of the church and receive prayer. But that instruction is for baby Christians who don't have much experience and haven't developed confidence.

Mark 16 makes it clear that we can all lay hands on people if we are believers. Instead of calling the church, a mature believer can lay hands on his wife and children when they need healing. A mature believer has confidence in his prayers and says, "Fine, the pastor can come for a visit and pray for my family while he is here, but I know what the Word says. I know that I am empowered to pray for my own family."

We need to rise above timidity and say, "I am going to step out and grab hold of this. I'm going to lay hands on the sick and pray."

"Just be Believing"

Luke 8 tells the story of Jairus, who is a director in the synagogue. Jairus' only daughter, a twelve-year-old child, is very sick, so Jairus comes to Jesus for help. While Jesus and Jairus are walking along the road toward Jairus' house, Jairus' friends run up to him and say, "Don't bother the Master any longer. Your daughter is dead."

If someone came up to you after church and said, "While you were in the church service, your daughter died. Just wanted you to know," you would be floored. Jairus gets such a message, and it overwhelms him too. But Jesus says, "Don't be alarmed. Simply believe."

The Greek words that are used in this passage are correctly translated, "Just be believing." That's what Jesus tells Jairus to do. He keeps walking toward Jairus' house, and He raises Jairus' daughter from the dead.

Jesus warned Jairus not to get into unbelief, which is believing that God can't do something He said He would do. Unbelief begins with the thought, "Yes, *but*... "

Jairus might have said, "Jesus said that He would heal my daughter. Yes, *but* now she is dead."

However, Jesus' message to Jairus was, "Don't give up your belief. Have enough confidence in Me to believe that I can heal her anyway."

To a modern believer, Jesus might say at that moment, "Just keep walking in faith."

Walking in faith means that you judge the things that come your way by what the Word says instead of by what you see.

Instead of saying, "*Yes*, I know what the Word of God says, *but* this is what I am seeing" you need to say, "Yes, I know what I am seeing, but the Word of God says..." See the difference? Now you're over into faith— you're saying what God says!

For instance, you might need a financial break-through. Although you don't have to deny that your wallet is empty, you say, "Yes, *but* God said, 'I will prosper you.'"

You might have a tumor. You don't have to deny that the tumor exists, but you need to keep your thoughts on

God's promises by saying, "Yes, *but* God has promised to heal me of sickness and disease."

Perhaps the school district has told you that your child has learning disabilities. You say, "Yes, *but* I know that God wants to bless us in all things, and I know that my family is blessed."

When we walk in faith, we are rooted, built up, and established in Him instead of being rooted, built up, and established in the things that we see.

Colossians 2:7 says, *"ROOTED and BUILT UP in him, and STABLISHED in the faith, as ye have been taught, abounding therein with thanksgiving."*

Rooted refers to our foundation, and *built up* refers to the finishing touches in our lives. When we are *established,* we are firm in our faith and cannot be moved. Being rooted, built up, and established in God is more important than most of us realize. It means that we are solid in God and will not be easily deceived.

Getting a Revelation of Christ in You

Smith Wigglesworth had a revelation of Christ *in him.* He used to say, "I am a thousand times bigger on the inside than I am on the outside."

On the outside, we are flesh, but on the inside we are supernatural beings, and our spirits are deep.

We often walk around feeling defeated, and Satan loves it when we are afraid. But if we could get a revelation of who we are spiritually, we would realize that we are spiritually huge and strong.

Christ is in us, and we are much stronger than we realize!

In Galatians 2:20, Paul says, "*I am crucified with Christ...*" In other words, he identifies with Christ on the Cross. And then he says, "*...nevertheless I live; yet not I, but Christ liveth **in me**: and the life which I now live in the flesh I live by the faith of the Son of God, who loved me, and gave himself for me.*"

When Jesus was on earth, Paul did not follow Him. In fact, Paul, a Pharisee named Saul at the time, thought Jesus' followers were blasphemers, and he persecuted them. He planned the stoning of Stephen and was on his way to Damascus to arrest Christians when he accepted Jesus Christ. When Jesus said to His disciples in Mark 16, "These signs shall follow you," Paul wasn't there.

Among the early believers, Paul never had the stature that Jesus' disciples had, and in 1 Corinthians 15:9, he said that he considered himself "the least of the apostles" because he had persecuted the Church. However, the same signs, wonders, and miracles that followed Peter, John, and the other disciples also followed Paul. Paul had the same power and authority that the twelve disciples had.

We don't have to be Jesus' twelve disciples to operate with power and authority. We do not have to be in the fivefold ministry or even be leaders in our church. Paul's life illustrates the truth that the signs are for every born-again believer and are not reserved for a special, chosen few.

Paul had a revelation of Christ in him, and we need to have that revelation too. We are complete in Christ, according to Colossians 2. All of Christ is within us, and when we realize that He is in us, we begin to live differently. Satan doesn't frighten us anymore.

Colossians 1:26 and 27 says, *"Even the mystery which hath been hid from ages and from generations, but now is made manifest to his saints: To whom God would make known what is the riches of the glory of this mystery among the Gentiles; which is CHRIST IN YOU, the hope of glory."*

"Christ in you" is the great mystery that was hidden from generations of Old Testament believers, but has been revealed to us.

The Infilling

First John 4:13 says, *"Hereby know we that we dwell in him, and he in us, because he hath given us of his Spirit."*

In other words, the Holy Spirit's Presence in our lives is our evidence that God is present with us. When John wrote the Book of First John, there was no controversy among Christians regarding the baptism in the Holy Spirit, and all believers were Spirit-filled. John is saying that the baptism in the Holy Spirit, with all of the power and signs that it brings, is our way of knowing that He lives in us.

First John 4:16 reminds us that love is a vital part of our walk. It says, *"And we have known and believed the love that God hath to us. God is love; and he that dwelleth in love dwelleth in God, and God in him."*

The word "dwelleth" is very important. It means that God is so committed to us that He makes His home in our lives and remains with us, no matter how challenging our lives may become.

The next verse, verse 17, is the verse that I want to focus on. It says, *"Herein is our love made perfect, that we may have boldness in the day of judgment: because as he is, so are we in this world."*

The last part of that verse says, *"...as he is, so are we in this world."* Well, how is He? Is He tired, discouraged, or confused? Is His schedule out of control? Does He have a cold? Is He running a fever? Does He have a stack of unpaid bills on the floor by His throne? Is He having a bad day?

Of course not! He is as solid as can be. And, according to 1 John 4:17, *". . . As He is, so are we in this world."*

Sometimes, we have a "big devil, little me" mentality, but God wants us to think differently. The devil is defeated, and we have the victory. Christ is in you, and there is nothing in the universe that is bigger or more powerful than that!

CHAPTER NINE

HOW TO RECEIVE A REVELATION

It's a serious thing when a doctor tells you that you have six months to live, and it's also a serious thing when you look in your checkbook and discover that you can't pay your rent.

When you face this kind of trouble, you need a revelation, and God wants to give a revelation to you.

Revelation is an uncovering or an unveiling. It is the moment when God shows us truths and realities that we could never discover for ourselves. Receiving a revelation from God is one of the most exciting parts of Christianity.

Perhaps you attend a church that teaches healing. If someone asks you, "Does God heal?" you answer immediately, "Oh, yes. God is a good God, and it is God's will to heal." In your mind, you know that God heals because of what you've heard taught. But one day, knowledge of healing explodes on the inside of you. Suddenly, God shows you truths about healing that you never knew before. You feel like the Holy Spirit just took the lid off the cookie jar! For you, healing is no longer a casual understanding. It has become a powerful reality. Revelation has come.

Sometimes people have the attitude, "The preacher gets revelation, but I don't know how to get it. And even if I did, I'd never get it anyway." But the Word of God says that anyone who hears the preaching of the Word can get a revelation from God.

Of course, I am not talking about something weird. The Bible warns us to stay away from teachings that are outside the Word. Colossians 2:8 says that spiritual messages which cannot be confirmed by Scripture are "vain deceits," and the Greek word used for deceit in this verse implies, *someone who hallucinates.*

However, scriptural revelation is a powerful, valid aspect of Christianity.

I heard one minister say that all you need is one word from the Lord. This means that a revelation from God can get you through anything. If you get a revelation about one Bible verse, it can get you healed.

Some people think, *Yes, revelation is wonderful, but it takes a long time to get a revelation. If I read the Bible for one hour every day and meditate, meditate, meditate, then maybe, after ten or fifteen years, I will get a revelation from God.*

Certainly, you should read the Bible on a daily basis and meditate on the verses that God's Spirit emphasizes to you. As Christians, we need a solid foundation from the Word. However, Paul, who wrote two-thirds of the New Testament by divine revelation, says that revelation does not come through meditation. It comes differently. Revelation does not require years of preparation. It is not hard to receive.

In fact, I have received revelation while I was lying in my bed at night, not praying or meditating at all. I would just be lying there, and God would reveal divine truths to me.

God gives revelation through His Holy Spirit. And if we are hungry for truth, revelation comes.

Getting a Word from the Lord

When I first got saved, I had such a desire for the Word that I read the Bible for three or four hours a day, and God revealed things to me. I wrote everything in notebooks, and I still have those notebooks today.

Of course, when I read them now, they are not revelation to me. Years have passed, and I have become well established in certain areas of the Word.

However, the truths that I wrote about were revelation to me then.

I had a lot of zeal, but my zeal wasn't tempered the right way. I would find things in the Word and would say, "I want to have a corner on this revelation, and I'm not going to share it with anyone."

I wanted to be able to say to people, "I know, but you don't." I was showing my spiritual immaturity.

God does not want to have a corner on the truth or hold secrets in Heaven. He does not say, "I'm not willing to share this with anyone." And He is not saying, "I'm saving this for a select few."

God is love, and His love is the love that gives. His nature is directed toward giving us the truth. And when He reveals something to us, He doesn't want us to keep it to ourselves. He wants us to bless other people by teaching it to them.

When I talk about revelation, I am not talking about understanding something that no one has received before. Ecclesiastes 1:9 says that there is nothing new under the sun, and everything God is revealing today is something He has revealed before. *Revelation always lines up with the written Word.*

However, when I talk about revelation, I am talking about the moment when a scriptural truth comes alive to you and begins to flow out of your heart to give you understanding and to bless you.

How Do You Get Revelation?

Paul was filled with revelation. He wrote two-thirds of the New Testament through divine revelation and had more revelation than any of us.

In Ephesians 1:15 and 16, Paul says, *"Wherefore I also, after I heard of your faith in the Lord Jesus, and love unto all the saints, Cease not to give thanks for you, making mention of you in my prayers."*

In other words, Paul heard that the Ephesians had gotten saved, and he remembered them in his prayers.

Ephesians 1:17 and 18 says, *"That the God of our Lord Jesus Christ, the Father of glory, may give unto you the spirit of wisdom and REVELATION in the knowledge of him: The eyes of your understanding being enlightened; that ye may know what is the hope of his calling, and what the riches of the glory of his inheritance in the saints."*

In Ephesians 1:17, the word "spirit" is the Greek word for the Holy Spirit, and the word should be capitalized. Verse 17 tells us that wisdom and revelation come from the Holy Spirit. Often, people try to get wisdom and revelation by memorizing Scripture or getting knowledge from the natural realm. But the Spirit of God is the only source for spiritual wisdom and divine revelation.

In this same verse, the word "revelation" simply means, *to be able to see.* It's like a curtain that is closed. All of a sudden, the curtain opens, and you can see to the other side.

When God, through His Holy Spirit, brings revelation, He opens things up to you.

God is Not Holding Back

The Word is revealed knowledge, and God wants us to know the Word. There is nothing in the Bible that God wants to keep secret from us.

Mark 4:11 says that the Kingdom of God is a mystery to people who are not born again. When they read the Bible, they say, "I don't get it." Everything has to be presented in parables to them.

However, in the same verse, Jesus says to the disciples, *"...Unto you it is given to KNOW the mystery of the kingdom of God..."*

The word "know" means, *to be sure of* and *to understand.*

Certainly, if Jesus wanted the disciples to know some things, He wants us to know them too.

Occasionally, I talk to Christians who say, "I'm ignorant about certain things in the Bible. I don't know much about healing, and I think God *wants* me to be ignorant. 'Let the ignorant be ignorant'—isn't that what the Bible says?"

The scriptural truth about healing has been revealed in Christ and is available to any believer who is willing to dig for it in the Bible. If you are ignorant about healing, it's because you have not made the effort to study the Word.

Romans 16:25 and 26 says, *"Now to him that is of power to stablish you according to my gospel, and the preaching of Jesus Christ, according to the revelation of the mystery, which was kept secret since the world began, But now is made manifest, and by the scriptures of the prophets, according to the commandment of the everlasting God, made known to all nations for the obedience of faith."*

This Scripture tells us that one of the ways revelation comes to us is by the Word. Someone is preaching, and, suddenly, revelation comes. Recently, while my wife, Barb, was preaching on a Sunday night, I began to receive revelation. As she taught, I wrote down the revelation I received.

Revelation is not limited to the Bible teacher, and understanding won't come from any source if you don't seek it. However, if you go after it, revelation will come.

There are times when a revelation will come, and it is one that brings correction. The Holy Spirit will reveal to you something in your life that needs to change.

For example, I may not be thinking about healing, when, out of the blue, a revelation comes. A light is turned on, and I know that I am not being healed because I have a bad attitude. Suddenly I realize, "That's it!"

Correction is not usually the revelation people are seeking, so often times they react by saying, "That can't be God. That must be the enemy." They ignore the correction, and healing doesn't come.

I want to emphasize that receiving a revelation of the Word of God is not hard. There are times when the Lord opens up something for me, and I get an entire sermon in five minutes' time. Of course, I need to study it out after that, but God's desire is to reveal things to us.

"Lord, I Need a Revelation!"

In Daniel 2, the Babylonian king, Nebuchadnezzar, has a disturbing dream. He can't remember the details of the dream, but is so agitated that he can't sleep. He calls in all of his magicians, enchanters, soothsayers, astrologers, sorcerers, and diviners and says, "Tell me what I dreamed and give me the interpretation, or I'll have you cut into pieces and your houses destroyed."

All the diviners and sorcerers say, "What you're asking for, we can't do. No one could show you these things except the gods, but they do not dwell with men."

The king becomes angry and commands that all of the wise men in the kingdom be killed.

Then Daniel goes before the king and says, "If you will tell me the time of your dream, I will interpret it."

Daniel goes back to his house and tells everything to Shadrach, Meshach, and Abednego, his Jewish companions. Daniel will die if he doesn't get this revelation, and so he prays to God.

Daniel 2:19 says, *"Then was the secret revealed unto Daniel in a night vision. Then Daniel blessed the God of heaven."*

Daniel goes back to the king and says, "The secret that the king has demanded to know, the diviners and sorcerers cannot reveal. But there is a God in Heaven who reveals secrets." And Daniel interprets Nebuchadnezzar's dream.

Visions aren't very popular among Christians today. In fact, if the Lord gives you a vision and you tell people about it, they usually think you're a flake. But God still wants to do supernatural things in His Church, and He is willing to give visions to people who seek Him.

At another time in the Old Testament, God reveals secrets to the prophet, Elijah. A group of kings is planning to attack Israel. One night, in his bedchamber, the king of Syria shares these secret plans with his closest advisors, and Elijah picks the plans up by the Holy Spirit. He goes to the king of Israel and says, "Watch out for this. This is going to happen."

The Israeli army ambushes the Syrian army, and the king of Syria says, "Who is telling secrets from my bedchamber?"

His leaders reply, "No one. There's this Jewish man who is a prophet. He hears these things by the power of his God, and then tells them to the King of Israel."

In our day, we don't have to be prophets to receive secret things by the Spirit. As we hunger after the Word, God will show us things. God revealed secrets to Daniel and Elijah, and He wants to do the same for us.

Sometimes, people come to me and say, "I have this lump on my body. Should I go to the doctor, or should I stand in faith?"

I always tell them, "I would go to the doctor."

Perhaps you're thinking, *That's not faith.* But if you are unsure enough to ask my advice, then working through a doctor is your level of faith, and that is not a bad thing. God will work with you wherever you are.

Perhaps, instead of going to the doctor, you say, "I am not going to the doctor, even though I have a lump on my body. I refuse to worry about this thing. I'm just believing what Pastor Mike preaches."

That's great. But my question to you is this: Are you doing it because I said it, or because God revealed it to you and *you know that you know that you know*?

If you are simply repeating what you've heard me say, then you'll be knocked flat if you get a bad medical report. But if God has given you a revelation, you'll be able to withstand any negative circumstance without wavering, and your faith will stay strong.

The Holy Spirit as a Revealer

John 16:13 says that the Holy Spirit will *"...shew you things to come."* In the Greek, the verse says, "He will reveal future events *in detail."*

From the Day of Pentecost, when He was first loosed on the earth, the Holy Spirit's job has been to reveal things to the Church.

First Corinthians 2:6 says, *"Howbeit we speak wisdom among them that are perfect: yet not the wisdom of this world, nor of the princes of this world, that come to nought."*

Paul was saying that he speaks wisdom among those who are maturing in the Lord, but he doesn't speak the wisdom of this world, and he doesn't speak the wisdom of the devil, who is the prince of this world.

Paul said in this verse that the devil has "come to nought," which means that he has been rendered powerless. The original Greek text says that Satan's forces have been put on idle. The only way Satan can be powerful is when we empower him by not having revelation of who we are in Christ.

First Corinthians 2:7-10 says,

But we speak the wisdom of God in a mystery, even the hidden wisdom, which God ordained before the world unto our glory: Which none of the princes of this world knew [In other words, this wisdom is meant for us.]: *for had they known it, they would not have crucified the Lord of glory. But as it is written, Eye hath not seen, nor ear heard, neither have entered into the heart of man, the things which God hath prepared for them that love him. But God hath revealed them unto us by his Spirit: for the Spirit searcheth all things, yea, the deep things of God.*

Everything in this passage is good, and these verses make it clear that knowing and understanding the things of God is very important, but the key phrase concerning revelation is in verse 9: "*...Eye hath not seen, nor ear heard, neither have ENTERED INTO THE HEART OF MAN, the things which God hath prepared for them that love him.*"

Your eye has not seen, and your ear has not heard, but, all of a sudden, it "*...entered into the heart of man...*" Suddenly, you've got it! Revelation enters your heart.

First Corinthians 2:9 says that God has prepared wonderful things for those who love Him. Healing, prosperity, peace, and righteousness—He has prepared all of these things for us. They are freely given.

Why, then, has the Church not received them?

We haven't received them because the Holy Ghost has not revealed them to us.

If the job of the Holy Ghost is to reveal things, why hasn't He revealed them? Why haven't they entered our hearts?

He hasn't revealed them to us because we haven't done something important. We haven't done a very critical part. We haven't prayed in tongues.

"Oh," you say, "Not *that*. Not tongues. That's the subject that splits churches and causes Christians to fight. Just talking about it causes controversy. Maybe we shouldn't even mention the need for tongues."

However, praying in tongues is the key to revelation. Other than salvation and calling on the Name of the Lord, I have never found anything as important to my Christian growth as praying in tongues. While I am praying in tongues—*boom*—things start to go off in my spirit. Revelation comes.

When you get a revelation from God, it excites you. It makes you want to run and shout. On the inside, you feel like a floodlight just came on. It is an exciting experience.

The Bible says that anyone who hears the Word can receive a revelation from God. It isn't a hard thing to do because God wants to give a revelation to you. It is spiritual life; it is a matter of the heart. It is the moment when the Holy Spirit opens something up to you. If you are hungry for revelation, you need to pray in tongues. The more you pray in the Spirit, the more you receive. God *wants* you to receive a revelation from Him.

Chapter Ten

Revelation Comes One Step at a Time

I watch unhappy Christians all the time. They don't have enough money to buy the things they want, they don't like their jobs, and they feel sick most of the time. They are sad when they are at home, and they are gloomy when they are at church. They are *miserable,* and they communicate their misery to everyone.

Christ is *in* them. If they had a revelation about who they are in Christ, they wouldn't be struggling. They would be walking in victory.

They are miserable because of the things they don't know.

They may go to a counselor, but he or she can't give them a revelation pill and say, "Swallow this." A counselor can't get them to know.

They may come to me. If I could pour revelation into their hearts the way I pour a quart of oil into the engine of my car, I would pour it in. But I can't get them to know, either.

They need knowledge and understanding, but the only One who can give them the knowledge they need is the Spirit of God.

Certainly, the Lord may use me to say something they need to hear, but the Holy Spirit is the only One who can unveil the truth to them.

The good news of the Bible is that He wants to give it to them. In fact, He is more eager to give than they are to receive. He is hungry to give them revelation. He *wants* them to know!

First Corinthians 2:9 says that God wants revelation to "enter into our hearts."

Jesus has done many things for us. And God, by the Holy Ghost, is *always* in the process of revealing those things to us. Sometimes we get upset with ourselves when we are struggling in an area instead of experiencing victory. We say, "I should be doing better than this."

However, we should focus on this: God *wants* us to know. If we are hungry for revelation, we simply need to find out what we are supposed to do in order to get it and then trust that revelation will come.

Who Gives Revelation?

If we are outside of Christ, we look for revelation in philosophy, education, and other places. We put our trust in the "wisdom of the world."

The world has a type of wisdom, but God has better wisdom, and He wants to share His wisdom with us. He reveals it to us by His Holy Spirit, according to 1 Corinthians 2:10.

People often say, "We need to get to know the Holy Ghost; that's how wisdom comes."

The Holy Spirit is living on the inside of us, and we certainly want to have a friendship with Him. However, we also need to know the *process* that He uses to communicate with us.

The Need for the Word

When I meet someone who is trusting God for a miracle, one of the first questions I ask him is, "What part of the Word are you standing on? Which Bible verses has God illuminated for you?"

I know that if there is no Word, there will be no breakthrough. Our first step in receiving revelation is to study the Word.

We say, "Holy Ghost, reveal something to me," but God doesn't bring revelation unless we have some Word in our lives. He needs to have something to work with.

This is the place where a lot of people get flaky. They want God to reveal things to them, and they really try to seek Him, but they don't have any Word in them. They begin to hear and believe things that did not come from God. The Word keeps you balanced and protects you from being deceived.

Two Sets of Eyes

We each have a set of eyes on our face, but Ephesians 1:18 says that we have a second pair of eyes.

They are on the inside of us, and they are the eyes of our understanding, or the eyes of our heart.

In Ephesians 1:18, Paul tells the Ephesians that he has asked God to open the eyes of their understanding. *The Amplified Bible* says that Paul has asked God to flood their eyes with light.

When the eyes of our understanding are opened, according to Ephesians 1:18 and 19, we begin to know and understand three things. *First*, we begin to know the hope to which God has called us. *Second*, we begin to know the glory of our rich inheritance. *Third*, we begin to understand the exceeding greatness of His power.

Paul started the Church at Ephesus and placed Timothy over it as pastor. When Paul wrote the book of Ephesians, the Ephesian church had approximately one hundred thousand members, which is a big church! Obviously, Paul prayed often for the Church at Ephesus. In Ephesians 1:18, he says, "I am praying for your church right now. I am praying for all of you collectively. And I am asking God to open the eyes of your understanding so that you will be able to see."

When our spiritual eyes are opened, we begin to *see* the things that Jesus has provided for us, such as healing and prosperity. We begin to *see* how God's principles can work in our marriages and our other relationships. We begin to *see* how we can walk in wholeness and peace. We begin to know and understand.

People say, "Well, I *don't* see. I tried memorizing some Scriptures, and I meditated on them, but they didn't open *my* spiritual eyes."

Meditating on and memorizing Bible verses is nice, but the eyes of our understanding are not opened that way. The eyes of our understanding are opened through prayer.

So we see the process. We study the Word. We get it into our hearts. Now God has something to work with.

Next, we pray, asking God to open the eyes of our understanding, or our hearts, so that we can begin to see into His Kingdom with the same clarity that we see into the natural realm.

God answers our prayers by giving us *"the spirit of wisdom and revelation in the knowledge of Him,"* according to Ephesians 1:17.

We already saw that the word "spirit" in Ephesians 1:17 is the Greek word for the Holy Spirit. In other words, when we ask God to open the eyes of our understanding, He instructs the Holy Spirit to give us two things: wisdom and revelation. *Wisdom* is insight and understanding. It is the ability to hear the Word and then apply it to our lives. *Revelation* is the moment when the Holy Spirit unveils spiritual truths that were concealed from us before. It is the moment when we say, "I see!"

When we ask God to open the eyes of our understanding, He uses the ministry of the Holy Spirit to apply wisdom and revelation to the Word that we've put on the inside.

Often, people say, "If Christ is in me, and I have all knowledge because He is there, then why do I need spiritual eyes? Why are they there?"

If we are believers, and if Christ is in us, it's true that everything in Jesus is sitting inside of us.

Certainly, all of it is there, but having it and seeing it are two different things. Having it and understanding it are two different things too.

For example, you can have a room full of electronic equipment—a big-screen television, a CD player with huge speakers, and a rack filled with great CDs. All of them can be sitting there, but if your room is dark, you won't understand that they're there. You may trip over them or crash into them as you try to walk around in the dark, but you certainly won't use them.

Revelation floods the room with light so that you can see the CD player, the CDs, and the television. Wisdom gives you the knowledge and understanding you need to use them. They were there all the time, but you didn't get any benefit from them until revelation and wisdom came.

You Need to Follow the Rules

God has given us a process for receiving revelation, and we need to follow the steps. We can compare His system with computer software that many of us use. For example, I have a Bible program on my computer. I have paid a software company for certain services, and these services are stored on a CD that was sent to me through the mail. The software company also sent me a number, or a code, that unlocks the services I paid for.

For example, I paid for the *King James Version* of the Bible with a corresponding Greek concordance. If I put the CD into my computer and type in my number, it unlocks the part of the CD that stores the *King James Version* with a Greek concordance. I have access to that.

Many other services are stored on the CD, but I didn't pay for those services, so I don't have a number that unlocks that information, even though the information is there.

If I purchase those services, the software company will give me new numbers, and the new numbers will unlock those other features, making them available to me.

Before I get the information, I need to pay the price.

Many Christians want the numbers, but they don't want to pay for the services.

In other words, many Christians want wisdom and understanding, but they don't want to go through the process of reading the Word and praying. But God does not give you revelation until you go through the process that the Bible has outlined for you.

One of the most important aspects of the process is this: God gives you the Spirit of wisdom and revelation in the knowledge of *Him*. We are not talking about knowledge of Buddha, Confucius, or Mohammed. We are not talking about the knowledge that is stored in libraries. Wisdom comes from the knowledge of God, and the only way to get knowledge of Him is to study the Bible.

In Ephesians 1:18, the Greek word that is used for knowledge is *"epignosis,"* which means, *exact and clear knowledge.* In other words, when we study the Bible, we begin to see God's knowledge in a very precise and accurate way. The word we often use for this knowledge is the word "enlightenment," which means that the light was turned on and the things that were once shadowy or unobservable are now crystal clear.

Perhaps you are at a time in your life when your marriage is a struggle. Maybe you think that applying the principles of Scripture to your marriage is like stumbling around in the dark.

In order to have a successful marriage, you need enlightenment about the principles of a happy marriage.

If you continue to take the Word in on a constant basis—not just at church, and if you continue to pray, asking God to open the eyes of your understanding, the light will come on, and you'll stop stumbling. God's knowledge about marriage will begin to be crystal clear.

Authority, Revelation, and Going to God

As soon as I get saved, Christ is in me, and all of God is in Christ. When it comes to authority and the devil, I don't have to grow in anything. I can be a newborn Christian, and if I resist the devil, he has to listen to me.

However, when it comes to revelation, I have to grow. I have to do everything that I have been taught to do.

There are times when I am doing everything that I know to do, and revelation still doesn't come.

So I say to God, "I need to be healed, but I'm not getting healed. I must be doing something to block my healing. Could you show me what it is, please?"

And God answers my prayer by saying, "You're in strife with So-and-so. You need to repent. That's why you aren't healed."

When I repent, my healing comes.

Many times, we can have sin in our lives for a while and still be okay, but the time finally comes when God confronts us. He says, "You have to quit being so hard on your wife. You can't treat her that way anymore."

Or maybe He says, "You've been watching soap operas, and you need to quit watching them."

These instructions don't come from other people. They come from the Holy Ghost. If we want God's blessings to flow in our lives, we need to make the adjustments that His Spirit instructs us to make.

Every day, Christians run to other people. They tell someone else all kinds of private details about themselves and then ask, "What adjustments do I need to make? What do you think I should do?"

In spiritual matters that concern their walk with God, they ask other people instead of asking God.

If I need the eyes of my understanding to be flooded with light, I'm not going to go to another person. I don't want another man's opinions. Instead, I am going to go into my bedroom, close the door, fall on my face before God, and ask Him what *He* thinks. And if He shows me that I need to repent or make other adjustments in my life, I'll do those things. But I don't really want someone else to know the details of my life, and God doesn't want that for me, either.

Most of the time, when we run to other people, it's because we asked God for help and didn't get it right away. We need to know that if we ask God to show us how to change our lives, He *will* answer us. His wisdom *will* come.

Prayers from the New Testament

Colossians is sometimes called the twin Epistle of Ephesians because the two letters were written around the same time.

In Colossians 1, Paul prays for the believers at Colossae. He asks God to give them wisdom and understanding, and his prayer is very similar to the prayer in Ephesians 1.

In Colossians 1:9 and 10, Paul says, *"For this cause we also, since the day we heard it, do not cease to pray for you, and to desire that ye might be FILLED WITH THE KNOWLEDGE OF HIS WILL in all wisdom and SPIRITUAL UNDERSTANDING; That ye might walk worthy of the Lord unto all pleasing, being fruitful in every good work, and increasing in the knowledge of God."*

"Filled" means, *to cram* or *to stuff.* "Of his will" in the Greek means, *to become one with one's wishes or with someone else's desire.*

"Spiritual understanding" means that spiritual truths begin to come together. Your eyes open, and you say, "I see. This truth fits into that area, and this truth goes over there." Everything begins to fit together.

In other words, Paul prays that the Colossians might overflow with the knowledge of God's wishes and desires and become one with His will for their lives.

The prayers in Ephesians and Colossians would be good prayers for church members to pray for their pastors, their bosses, and other people in positions of authority.

Ask God to cram them with knowledge of His will in *all* wisdom so that they will be able to apply God's knowledge to every situation. Ask Him to give them spiritual understanding so that all of the facts come together. Ask God to help them to walk worthy so that they are living right and doing the right thing.

Paul goes on to say in verse 10, *"...unto all pleasing, being fruitful in every good work..."* Asking God to make your boss fruitful in every good work would be a wonderful prayer!

Often, when we are frustrated with people or we don't like them, we try to change them with our prayers. "God, make that pastor do what *I* want him to do," we pray. Or, "Change my boss, Lord. Tell him to be the boss that I need him to be." Or, "Turn my husband into the man I want him to be."

God is up in Heaven saying, "You're kidding! I don't want to turn him into the man *you* want him to be. I am trying to get him to do it *My* way."

If we pray Paul's prayers from Ephesians 1 and Colossians 1 for the people in our lives, and if we pray other verses for them that God reveals to us, we won't get off track, and our prayers will bless their lives.

"Lord, Help Me See"

Some people think that they are being selfish when they pray for themselves, but we are not being selfish when we pray, "Lord, help me see." In fact, when the eyes of our understanding are opened, we begin to see the way Christ sees, and selfishness goes away.

It won't hurt for you to pray, "Lord, open my eyes. Open my heart." In fact, it would be a good thing.

Perhaps you have a hard time walking in love. You could pray, "Lord, I don't see love like the Word says to love. I have a hard time loving certain people. Help me here." The key word in this kind of praying is the word "comprehend," which means, *to lay hold of* or *to obtain*. We pray, "Lord, if I could start comprehending this [laying hold of it, understanding it], I know that everything would change. Lord, help me to comprehend."

Comprehending Healing

Laying hold of healing is one of the things that we need to pray about. For some of us, healing is hard to comprehend.

We need to pray, "Lord, open my eyes to healing." "Help me to lay hold of the understanding that Jesus heals."

Certainly, I did not lay hold of the truth that Jesus is a healer right away. The revelation of Jesus the Healer came to me step by step as I sought Him and applied myself to His Word and to prayer.

The Process

We have learned that we need revelation, which comes from the Holy Spirit. We don't get everything in one day. Instead, we go through a process. We begin by studying the Word. We read it at church and at home. On a daily basis, we put it into our hearts.

Then we move on to prayer. We say, "Lord, I am believing that You will open the eyes of my heart. I need to see some things."

God's Holy Spirit answers our prayers by applying wisdom and revelation to the Word that we've put in our hearts. He helps us by showing us things.

Of course, we need to be holy. We need to obey God's Holy Spirit when He instructs us to change.

As we follow the steps in the process, the Holy Spirit will unveil the truth, the eyes of our understanding will see the things that God has provided for us, and revelation will come.

CHAPTER ELEVEN

HEALING: GOD'S VARIOUS BATTLE PLANS

Recently, I went to Guatemala, and while I was there, I began to hate the devil more than I have ever hated him.

Everywhere I looked, I saw people who were suffering from sickness and poverty.

Some of us think that our lives are hard, and there are pockets of ignorance and poverty in the United States, but no one in this country deals with the oppression and suffering that is rampant in other parts of the world.

The Gospel has been preached powerfully in the United States for over three hundred years, and we send out nine of every ten missionaries in the world, so God has blessed us. We don't really know what poverty is.

In other parts of the world, a spirit of poverty hangs over people's lives, and there are nations on this earth that are terribly oppressed.

The saddest part of the suffering is that God wants people to be blessed.

God wants us to have money in our pockets and hearts that are full of hope. He wants us to have strong bodies and good health. When you go to a country that is crippled with poverty, you usually find a spiritual root. In the countries that used to be Communist, for example, there is darkness and poverty because of the spiritual forces that were at the root of Communism. These spiritual forces tried to rule over these countries and keep them in poverty.

Thank God for America! We have drifted toward secularism in the last fifty years, and in some ways our protective hedge has come down, but we still have a sense of safety in this country that other countries don't have.

Unfortunately, we also have religious people who run around saying, "God makes you sick." That's a shame. God does not make us sick. It's the last thing He wants to do.

Red and Yellow, Black and White

God made each of us different. We all know how it is. One person is crying at a movie, and the other person is thinking, *What's wrong with you?* Certain things get to me that wouldn't get to you.

Some people receive healing easily when they pray, and others need to go through a healing line. Different methods work for different people, so God made many different ways for people to be healed.

Different Battle, Different Plan

Acts 19:11 and 12 says, *"And God wrought special miracles by the hands of Paul: So that from his body were brought unto the sick handkerchiefs or aprons, and the diseases departed from them, and the evil spirits went out of them."*

In our church, we sometimes lay hands on handkerchiefs. Church members give these handkerchiefs to sick friends and relatives and say, "Leave this on you, and you will be healed." Often, the people who get the handkerchiefs are unsaved people who don't want to come to our church.

Many people have been healed after using these handkerchiefs. They have been cured of cancer and other terminal illnesses.

This is one of God's ways of bringing healing into people's lives.

Of course, God has a different way of dealing with every situation. In the Old Testament, when David was the king of Israel, the Israelite army fought many battles. Often, David faced situations that were very similar to battles he'd fought in the past. However, he never depended on past experience. He always asked God, "How do you want us to fight this battle?" Every time, God gave David a different battle plan.

When we are sick, we need to follow David's example and say, "God, I need to be healed, but I'm not going to do anything until You show me the method You want me to use. I'm not going to have hands laid on me, and I'm not going to try to get a cloth. I'm going to wait on You."

And God might say to you, "Have hands laid on you."

So you go to the elders of your church so that they can anoint you with oil, lay hands on you, and pray for your healing. And while they are praying, you are filled with confidence because the Lord has told you that when hands are laid on you, you will be healed.

Handkerchiefs

The anointing has the ability to go into cloth. Our sanctuary has a lot of cloth on the floor, the chairs, and the walls. When the room is full of believers, anointing is drawn out of them, and it goes into all of the cloth.

I often walk around and pray in the sanctuary of my church because I can feel the anointing from all the services we've had in that room.

Sometimes, people are healed when they sit down on the upholstered chairs. They say, "Whoa, I just got healed!" They're healed because they believe Acts 19:11 and 12 and realize that it's possible to be healed by anointed cloth.

One day, a woman who is a member of my church came to me after a service, held out a cloth, and asked me to lay hands on it. She said, "My husband is not saved, and I want to put this cloth inside his pillow case. Every night, when he lies on this cloth, I believe that the power of God will go into him and that he will be saved." In other words, she believed God for salvation rather than for healing. That's where her faith was, and she was very confident about it.

I laid hands on the cloth, and she took it home.

Three or four weeks later, her husband started coming to church with her. He had been saved—he accepted Jesus as his Savior—after sleeping on that cloth!

Perhaps you're thinking, *That poor guy was tricked, sleeping on that cloth.*

My response to you is, "Whatever it takes."

Here was a godly wife who thought, *I don't want my husband to die and go to hell. I want him to be saved.* She exercised her faith, and her husband found Jesus after sleeping on an anointed cloth. I'm sure he's not complaining about it today.

The Name of Jesus

Acts 3:1-16 tells the famous story of Peter and John with the crippled beggar at the temple gate in Jerusalem. John and Peter are going into the temple to pray, and the crippled man asks them for money. In Acts 3:6, Peter says, *"...Silver and gold have I none; but such as I have give I thee: In the name of Jesus Christ of Nazareth rise up and walk."*

It's one of my favorite Scriptures. I heard it when I first got saved, so I started walking up to people on crutches or in wheelchairs and saying it to them. Actually, there were a few times when I shouted it. I'd say, "I'm a Christian, so in the Name of Jesus, I'm commanding you to get up and walk."

They'd always look at me as if to say, "Are you crazy or what!"

After a while, I became depressed. I couldn't understand why people weren't throwing down crutches and jumping out of wheelchairs, like the man at the gate in Acts chapter 3.

There was a reason for it, and if we continue to read the story, we'll find out what the reason was.

Peter took the crippled man by the right hand and lifted him up. Immediately, the bones in his feet and ankles received strength. He stood up and began to leap around, praising God. He went into the temple with Peter and John, leaping, and praising God all the way.

Acts 3:16 says, *"And his name through faith in his name hath made this man strong..."*

The Name of Jesus is an avenue for healing. If you don't have any faith in Jesus' Name, you won't be healed, but if you put faith in the Name of Jesus, you can receive healing every single time. There are many ways to be healed, but this is one of the simplest ways.

Matthew 18:19 says, *"Again I say unto you, That if two of you shall agree on earth as touching any thing that they shall ask, it shall be done for them of my Father which is in heaven."*

This verse is talking about using the Name of Jesus. If two of you shall put your faith in the Name of Jesus and agree, asking, it will be done for you by God.

Of course, you can't give up on your faith. Sometimes, people get discouraged if they don't see an answer to their prayers after two or three days. They say, "I was believing for three days, and it didn't happen."

God is proud of you for standing in faith for three days, but three days is just a moment in the span of His timing, and He wants you to keep standing. The Bible says again and again, "Don't give up!"

Ephesians 6:13 says, *"Wherefore take unto you the whole armour of God, that ye may be able to withstand in the evil day, and having done all, to STAND."*

Often, we misunderstand Ephesians 6:13. When we think of standing, we think of a passive state.

"Stand" means, *to abide* or *to stay where you are.* You get to the place of withstanding the evil day by being full of faith. And when Satan pushes against your faith with doubt, deception, and trickery, you use every spiritual weapon that God has given you to hold your ground.

When pressure comes, you watch your mouth, guard your thoughts, and stay in your place of faith. The rest is up to God.

Speaking the Word

Luke 7 tells the story of the Roman centurion whose trusted servant is dying.

The centurion hears about Jesus and asks some Jewish religious leaders to go to Jesus on his behalf. The leaders tell Jesus that the centurion is a good man who has built them a synagogue.

Jesus goes with the Jewish leaders, but as He approaches the centurion's house, the centurion sends friends to Him with this message: *"...Lord, trouble not thyself: for I am not worthy that thou shouldest enter under my roof: Wherefore neither thought I myself worthy to come unto thee: but say in a word, and my servant shall be healed"* (Luke 7:6,7).

This Roman military officer trusts Jesus' Word, and Jesus marvels at his faith.

We have already looked at two methods by which God heals—handkerchiefs or cloth and the Name of Jesus. The centurion's story illustrates a third method of healing, which is speaking the Word.

It is said that this is the highest level of receiving healing. Many people are not yet at this level of faith, but the spoken Word can heal you.

Recently, I had problems with my legs. One day, while I was praying about the problem, the Lord said, "You're going to receive this healing by speaking," and that's how the healing came. I didn't have anyone lay hands on me and pray. Instead, I spoke healing Scriptures over my situation and received my healing by speaking the Word, which took me to a new level of faith.

Laying On of Hands and Anointing with Oil

James 5:14 says, *"Is any sick among you? let him call for the elders of the church; and let them pray over him, anointing him with oil in the name of the Lord."*

In this verse, James is writing to the Church. He is talking to believers who have done everything they know to do without getting good results and are beyond helping themselves. James instructs these believers to call their pastors so that the pastors can anoint them with oil and pray the prayer of faith.

The oil doesn't heal you. You could jump into a swimming pool full of oil and not be healed. Healing comes through the prayer of faith.

James 5:15 says, *"And the prayer of faith shall save the sick, and the Lord shall raise him up; and if he have committed sins, they shall be forgiven him."*

The word "save" in the Greek is the word "sozo," which means, *heal, deliver, protect, rescue,* or *save.* The prayer of faith will heal, deliver, protect, rescue, and save the sick one. God will respond to the prayer of faith by raising him up.

The laying on of hands with the anointing of oil is another way that God brings healing into people's lives, and the laying on of hands is the easiest way for people to be healed.

Hebrews 6:1 and 2 says that the laying on of hands is one of the six basic doctrines of the Church. It is the milk of the Word, which means that it is uncomplicated enough for a newborn Christian to receive by this means. Even a baby Christian can understand that if others touch him with their hands, he can receive healing through their touch.

When I deal with sick children, I usually minister by the laying on of hands. When I was in Guatemala, I ministered healing by the laying on of hands, and I watched healing flow to many.

Spiritual Gifts

First Corinthians 12 is the well-known chapter of the New Testament that talks about spiritual gifts. It teaches us that the gifts are diverse, but all of them are good, and the Spirit gives them to the Church so that they can empower and benefit us. They are another avenue for God's healing power.

Many times, we say of the gifts, "They're as the Spirit wills." Certainly, the Bible says that the Holy Spirit governs the spiritual gifts, but we make it sound as if the Spirit is unpredictable. "Well, maybe next week, if we're lucky, the Spirit will work in our church," we seem to say.

The Holy Spirit is part of God, and if someone is being destroyed by sickness, He is *always* willing to move. He's always willing to operate.

Of course, we have to learn to listen to the Holy Ghost. We can't run out ahead of Him and expect Him to follow us. We have to follow Him. If we are obedient enough to do whatever He empowers us to do, we can see some marvelous and stupendous results.

One time, Smith Wigglesworth walked up to an open coffin at a funeral home and threw the dead man onto the floor in front of his friends and relatives and commanded him in the Name of Jesus to live. The man came back to life! Of course, you have to be *sure* that you have heard from God before you try doing something like that. Otherwise, you might find yourself in a straightjacket somewhere. But if we are bold enough to do whatever God's Spirit anoints us to do, we may find ourselves doing some unconventional things.

An Example of Spiritual Gifts in Operation

First Corinthians 12:9 says that the "gifts of healing" is one of the spiritual gifts. The gifts of healing is a special anointing that can come on someone. However, you can personally receive healing without the gifts of healing being in operation, and you can minister healing to someone else without this spiritual gift.

If you have the Word in your heart, and if you have faith, you can be healed, and you can minister healing to someone else.

Several years ago, a member of my church went on a mission trip to Peru. He got sick, wasn't able to eat, and died. When the man died, the gift of faith came on another member of the mission team. He jumped on the dead man's body and commanded life to come back into him, and it did.

In order to raise someone from the dead, you need the gift of faith. When you are operating in this spiritual gift, you aren't moved by what you see, no matter what it is. Even if a person is dead, your faith is not shaken. It's almost like someone else is working and you're not really doing anything. That's because God is working through you.

You also need to operate in the gift of the working of miracles, which is identified in First Corinthians 12:10. Otherwise, you will bring the dead man back to life through the operation of the gift of faith, but he will die again due to whatever illness he succumbed to in the first place.

All of these spiritual gifts (the gifts of healing, the gift of faith, and the gift of the working of miracles) go into operation when someone is raised from the dead.

Unbelief Versus Trust and Belief

Have you ever noticed how easy it is to minister healing to people in Third World countries? They don't question the healing message, and they don't have doubts about the power of God. They simply reach out and receive.

The miraculous, healing power of God can be shut off by unbelief, and people in our country often think they are too sophisticated to be healed by cloths, Bible verses, prayers, or the laying on of hands. Jesus experienced this in Nazareth, His hometown.

Mark 6:5 says, *"And he could there do no mighty work, save that he laid his hands upon a few sick folk, and healed them."*

Jesus could not exercise His miraculous power and deliver people from death because the people of Nazareth did not believe.

All of God's "Battle Plans" Require Faith

God has provided a number of different ways for people to be healed. We can look at these different methods as God's "battle plans." People can be healed by anointed cloth and by the Name of Jesus. The prayer of faith, the operation of spiritual gifts, and the spoken Word can heal them. They can also be healed by the laying on of hands, which I said is probably the easiest way to receive healing.

If you believe that anointed cloths can't heal you, you will not be healed by them. If you don't believe in the power of the Name of Jesus, His Name won't bring healing to you. If you have no faith in spiritual gifts or in the Word, they won't bring you miracles. And if you don't think that healing can be transferred by the laying on of hands, you will not be healed, even if you are in a spiritually charged room.

Healing is available to those who believe.

If you believe that Jesus is your healer, and if you believe that the methods of healing that are outlined in the Bible are valid and dependable, then you can be healed right now.

CHAPTER TWELVE

GOD HAS GIVEN YOU HEALING POWER!

John 3:16 says, *"For God so loved the world, that he GAVE his only begotten Son, that whosoever believeth in him should not perish, but have everlasting life."*

Romans 8:32 says, *"He that spared not his own Son, but delivered him up for us all, how shall he not with him also freely GIVE us all things?"*

Matthew 7:9-11, says, *"Or what man is there of you, whom if his son ask bread, will he give him a stone? Or if he ask a fish, will he give him a serpent? If ye then, being evil* [or natural], *know how to give good gifts unto your children, how much more shall your Father which is in heaven give good things to them that ask him?"*

These are foundational Scriptures, that show us God loves us, gave His Son for us, and wants to give us *all* good things. God is a giving God, and the things that He gives us are good!

You and I are "evil," which simply means that we are natural, imperfect parents. But if our children say, "Mom and Dad, I'm hungry," we certainly wouldn't give them a stone. We'd run to our kitchen and get them some bread—something to eat.

If our children say, "I'm hungry for fish," we wouldn't give them a plate full of snakes. We would give them something good.

If we are able to love and give good things to our children, then God, who is our spiritual father, is much more able to love and give to us.

If we go to Him with sickness in our bodies, He doesn't say, "You know, you already have this sickness, but I think I'll give you more. Let me give you cancer too. It will teach you a lesson." God doesn't behave that way. That's not the kind of God we serve.

First Timothy 6:17 says that He gives us *"...all things to enjoy."*

James 1:5 says, *"If any of you lack wisdom, let him ask of God, that giveth to all men liberally, and upbraideth not; and it shall be given him."*

"Upbraid" means, *to scold.* James 1:5 says that if we ask God for wisdom, He will give us a generous amount of wisdom and will not scold us for needing it. This is good news!

These five scriptures—John 3:16, Romans 8:32, Matthew 7:9-11, 1 Timothy 6:17, and James 1:5—show that God is a giver. He gives love, good gifts, and wisdom. In fact, He gives us all good things, and He wants us to enjoy them! He loves us so much that He even gave us His Son.

In order to receive healing, we need to have it settled in our hearts that God is a giver and that He is willing to give us healing power.

There is no place in the Bible where people ask God to heal them and He says, "I can't heal you today. I'm only giving out deadly diseases today."

We cannot find a time in the New Testament when Jesus refuses to heal. This type of attitude is not in His character.

There is a passage in Matthew 15 where it seems that He doesn't want to heal someone. Jesus goes to the district of Sidon and Tyre, which is north of Israel, and as He is traveling, a woman from that region comes to him and cries in a loud and urgent way that her daughter is possessed by a demon. She begs for help. Jesus says, "...*I am not sent but unto the lost sheep of the house of Israel*" (Matt. 15:24).

The Canaanite woman falls at Jesus' feet and worships Him, but He replies, "It is not appropriate for Me to take the children's bread and throw it to the dogs" (v. 26).

The woman won't give up. She says, "Yes, Lord, but even the little puppies eat the crumbs that fall from their master's table."

Jesus is moved by the woman's faith. He says, "Oh, woman, great is your faith. *Be it done for you as you wish*" (v. 28). And the woman's daughter is cured from that moment.

The point of my sharing this story is that there is no place in the Bible where Jesus refused to heal someone who asked for His help. Everyone who asked Jesus for healing power was healed.

And He hasn't changed. If we say, "Lord, that's a wonderful blessing. I really want that," He says, "It's yours."

They Came to be Healed

Luke 6:17 says, *"And he came down with them, and stood in the plain, and the company of his disciples, and a great multitude of people out of all Judaea and Jerusalem, and from the sea coast of Tyre and Sidon, which came to hear him, and to be healed of their diseases."*

Some people think they're being gracious when they come to church without expecting anything from God. They say, "I'm not here to get anything. I'm just here to worship God."

However, it's a good thing to come to church with an attitude of expectancy. It pleases God! The people in Luke 6:17 had a purpose in coming to Jesus. They came to hear Jesus and to be cured.

Luke 6:18 and 19 says, *"And they that were vexed with unclean spirits: and they were healed. And the whole multitude sought to touch him: for there went VIRTUE out of him, and healed them all."*

The Greek word for virtue is "dunamis," which means, *miraculous healing power.* Look again at Luke 6:18 and 19. God's miraculous healing power was displayed to the great multitudes when Jesus "healed them all."

Perhaps you're saying, "Yes, Pastor, we see that Jesus healed everyone. It's very clear in the Word. But we aren't Jesus."

No, we're not Jesus, but as believers He dwells in us. Look at what Jesus says in John 14:12, *"Verily, verily I say unto you, He that believeth on me, the works that I do shall he do also..."* Mark 16:17 says, *"And these signs shall follow them that believe..."*

Virtue isn't something that was only available while Jesus was on earth, and it isn't something that we have to wait until we get to Heaven to receive. God has given us miraculous healing power, and it is His desire that His children walk in it. Healing power is for us today! It is available now.

You Have to *Release* Your Faith

Luke 6:19 says that the whole multitude sought to touch Jesus. They had probably heard about the woman with the issue of blood, and they believed that they would be healed when they touched Jesus. That's where their faith was—they placed their faith in touching Him.

Jesus often said, "Your faith has made you whole." Your faith is vital to your healing.

Faith is simply what you believe. Faith is the set of convictions that govern your life. *Vine's* translation says that faith is *conviction based upon what you believe.*

Romans 10:17 says, faith comes by hearing. Although we hear many things, we don't place our faith in everything we hear. Faith comes when we hear something and accept it as the truth.

For example, when I hear the Word, I start to believe it. I accept it as truth. Then, faith starts to come. The next step is to release my faith; I need to act on it. Many Christians have unreleased faith, and that's why they aren't healed.

Your Faith Plays a Part in Your Healing

Recently, I preached on healing, and we had visitors in the service who came to me afterward to tell me that they disagreed with what I said.

"God will heal when He wants to heal. If He doesn't want to heal, He won't. Faith has nothing to do with it," they said.

Throughout the New Testament, Jesus says, "Your faith has made you whole." But the Bible says that faith is a critical element in receiving blessings from the Lord.

Mark 11:24 says, *"Therefore I say unto you, What things soever ye desire, when ye pray, believe that ye receive them, and ye shall have them."*

In other words, when you have faith in God's Word, you believe that you receive healing before it is visible. You act like you have it, even though it hasn't manifested yet. That is faith!

For example, when you pray the prayer of faith in James 5:14-15, and believe that you're healed, you have received your healing even though you don't feel healed and may still have symptoms of the sickness or disease.

If you want to be healed, you have to get strong in this area. When a symptom comes, whether it's a cough, a headache, or something else, you can't accept the symptom. You can't let the symptom shake your belief. You are healed, no matter what your symptoms say. So you confess, "I'm standing against the symptom, and I am standing in faith. I am healed, in Jesus' Name." Your attitude should be that of a bulldog on a bone. You will not be moved until you get what you're believing for!

Getting a Little Exercise

We exercise our faith, just like we exercise our bodies. We don't want to run a marathon with weak muscles, and we don't want to face a health crisis with weak faith. We work out, so to speak, by using our faith to believe for smaller things.

For example, I used to get a lot of headaches. As soon as a headache started, I took a pain reliever. After awhile, the Lord began to deal with me. "Instead of trusting the pain reliever, trust Me," He began to say.

One night I got a headache, and instead of taking medication, I exercised my faith in God. I said, "I'm not going to take a pain reliever tonight. Instead, I'm going to stand in faith."

It was hard. Believing that God would heal my headache took all of the faith I had. But it was a little bit easier the next time, and it's really easy today. Now that I'm stronger in faith, I can believe God for bigger things.

Not Looking for Manifestations

Acts 10:38 says, *"How God anointed Jesus of Nazareth with the Holy Ghost and with power: who went about doing good, and healing all that were oppressed of the devil; for God was with him."*

God gave healing power to Jesus. That's the reason why everyone who came in contact with Jesus was healed.

When we go to God for healing, we are not looking for manifestations. We are looking for the *healing power* that operated through Jesus.

Sometimes, the symptoms don't go away immediately, but if hands are laid on us and healing power comes in, then we are healed, no matter how we feel, and we need to rejoice in that.

If you say, "I had hands laid on me today, but I don't look or feel any different. I guess I didn't get anything," you lose whatever it is that God wants to do in your life.

But you can hold on to your healing when you say, "I received healing power by the laying on of hands, and healing power is working in me. When I approach God in faith, He gives me healing power. I know that I am healed, no matter how I feel." Release your faith, and speak the end result (Rom 4:17).

Power That Can't be Driven Out

In the past, we were taught that unbelief would drive God's healing power out of a room. However, the healing power of Jesus is more powerful than the force of unbelief, and if Jesus finds a faith-filled man, He can bring healing, even if the room is filled with hostility and unbelief.

Luke 5:17-26 is the story of the paralyzed man who is healed by Jesus after his friends lower him through the roof.

Jesus is teaching, and there are Pharisees and doctors of the Law in the room. They have come out of every town of Galilee, Jerusalem, and Judea, and they believe that Jesus' power comes from the devil, so they are looking for a reason to have Him killed.

You can't face tougher opposition than that!

Nevertheless, *"...the power of the Lord was present to heal them"* (Luke 5:17).

The paralyzed man's friends are unable to find a way through the crowd, so they make a hole in the roof and lower the man's stretcher to the floor in front of Jesus. When Jesus sees their faith, He says to the man, "Your sins are forgiven" (v. 20).

The Pharisees and other religious leaders are outraged. They begin to reason, "This man speaks blasphemies. No one can forgive sins but God."

Jesus responds to their unbelief by asking, "Is it easier for me to say, 'Your sins are forgiven' or to tell this man to get up and walk? But so that you will know that the Son of God has the authority on earth to forgive sins, I say to this crippled man, 'Walk'" (vv. 23,24).

Immediately, the crippled man jumps up, grabs his stretcher, and goes home, praising God as he goes!

We learn several lessons from this story.

First of all, Jesus saw the faith of the sick man's friends, so we learn that faith can be seen. *Second*, we see that healing was available to the Pharisees and doctors of the Law, even though they didn't believe in Jesus. *Third*, we see that healing is connected with forgiveness and is part of the redemptive plan.

On the night I was saved, I remember thinking, *Believe, confess, and repent. Is that all that I have to do? That was easy.*

Salvation is easy, and healing is easy too. You believe in your heart and confess with your mouth, and healing comes to you.

Of course, salvation doesn't bring instant change in your circumstances. After you become a new man in your spirit, you walk out your salvation in your soul and in the natural realm. Salvation starts on the inside and works its way out. Healing works the same way. It begins in your heart and works its way into your natural circumstances.

The Woman Who Released Her Faith

In Mark 5, Jesus heals a woman who has an issue of blood. We have studied this passage before, but we'll look at it again. The woman has been hemorrhaging for twelve years, but she works her way through a crowd, touches the hem of Jesus' garment, and is healed.

She has heard the reports about Jesus and has accepted those reports as the truth, so she has *received* faith. When she leaves her home and goes through the crowd to touch Jesus, she *releases* her faith.

How does she release her faith? She acts. She moves. This is how faith is released.

As soon as she touches the garment of Jesus, her flow of blood dries up at its source, and she feels in her body that she has been healed of her ailment.

Multitudes are touching Jesus, but one person, through faith, draws healing power from Him.

When Jesus looks around to see who has done this thing, He doesn't say, "*My* faith has made you whole." He says, "*Your* faith has made you whole." The woman is healed because she released *her* faith.

Another Example of Releasing Faith

Recently, I heard the story of a couple that faced a cancer diagnosis. The woman was told that she had cancer.

The diagnosis hit this couple hard, and both of them could feel themselves getting into fear.

The husband said, "We're not going to talk about this yet. We're not even going to pray. Instead, we are going to get into the Word, and then we'll have the strength to do what we need to do."

For two weeks, this couple spent time in the Word and built up their faith. And then the husband laid hands on his wife and prayed. Instantly, she was healed.

The Power of Confession

Hebrews 4:14 says, *"Seeing then that we have a great high priest, that is passed into the heavens, Jesus the Son of God, let us hold fast our profession* [confession]."

This passage says that if you are a believer, you have to hold on to what you are speaking. You have to be careful about what you confess.

Our words have incredible power. In fact, the Old Testament says that the power of life and death is in our tongues (Prov. 18:21). If our words are empowered by the Word of God and the Holy Ghost, they have life in them, and when we speak an anointed word, things have to change!

In Mark 5:28 the woman with the issue of blood had a confession. She kept saying, "If I touch His garment, I will be made whole." As she was going through the crowd, she probably had to hold on to that confession. According to the Levitical law, she wasn't supposed to leave her house, so people probably spit on her and called her names.

She was weak, so she may have been pushed or even knocked down and stepped on. She had spent all of her money on doctors, so she was poor, and people probably looked at her and thought, *You dirty old rotten thing. Get out of this crowd.*

This woman didn't just breeze through the crowd, touch Jesus, and say, "Oh, I'm healed!" She faced a lot of adversity, but she held on to her confession.

Hebrews 10:23 says, *"Let us hold fast the profession of our faith without wavering; for he is faithful that promised."*

In other words, we have to hold on tight to our confession without faltering or changing directions because there's a spiritual force that is trying to make us let go, and we need to resist that force.

People have told me, "I confessed for two days that I was healed, but the symptoms didn't change, so I just gave up."

They didn't hold on tight to their confession. Instead, they wavered and changed direction. In order to see the manifestation of our healing, we have to hold on tight.

On several occasions, I've had to confess for months before I saw my healing. I just kept saying, "I'm healed by His stripes. I don't care what it looks like. I don't care how I feel. I am healed."

There were days when it wasn't easy for me to hold on to my confession, and there were days when I wanted to scream. There were even times when I wanted to say, "Where are You, God?"

Perhaps you've loosened the grip on your confession and said, "I guess I'm not healed after all." You need to destroy those words, asking God to forgive you for your unbelief.

Just keep reminding yourself that God is faithful, according to Hebrews 10:23. Whatever He promises, He will bring to pass.

In Your Heart and in Your Mouth

Romans 10:8 says, " ...*The word is nigh thee, even in thy mouth, and in thy heart* ..."

In other words, the Word resides in two places: the heart and the mouth.

Faith comes by the Word. When you study the Bible, faith gets into your heart. After that, faith comes out of your mouth. That's how faith is released.

Often, symptoms come, and we immediately say, "By His stripes I am healed. By His stripes I am healed." Most of us have done it. In those moments, we're reciting words; however, our words aren't filled with faith. But, when we take the time to get the Word into our hearts, we get our faith moving in the right direction. Then we can begin to speak faith-filled words. Faith-filled words bring God's power.

It's Simple

God, in His goodness, has given us various ways and methods by which we can receive His gift of healing, and He has made it simple. We have His Word that answers every question and lays to rest every doubt. By His Word, we have the comforting knowledge that it is always His will that we receive healing and walk in divine health.

Receiving healing isn't difficult. In fact, healing is very simple. Believe in your heart God's Word concerning healing, confess it with your mouth, and you will be healed!

"How Do I Get to Heaven?"

The Bible declares that we can know that we have eternal life. I John 5:13 reads, *"These things have I written unto you that believe on the name of the Son of God; that ye may know that ye have eternal life, and that ye may believe on the name of the Son of God."*

Acts 2:21 tells us that, *"...whosoever shall call on the name of the Lord shall be saved."* And Romans 10:9-10 (NKJV) reads, *"That if you confess with your mouth the Lord Jesus, and believe in your heart that God has raised Him from the dead, you will be saved. For with the heart one believes to righteousness; and with the mouth confession is made to salvation."*

Laying hold on eternal life is as simple as believing that Jesus Christ is the Son of God, that He died and was raised from the dead, and then confessing (or saying) that with your mouth. If you have never called on the Name of the Lord—don't put it off one more day. The following is a prayer of salvation. Read aloud this prayer and receive eternal salvation!

Prayer of Salvation

"Heavenly Father, I come to you in Jesus' Name. The Bible says that if I call on the name of the Lord, I will be saved. So, I do that now. I believe in my heart that Jesus came to the earth, was crucified, and rose from the dead. I confess that Jesus is Lord. I thank you that I am now a Christian—a child of God! I am saved and have received eternal life."

If you just prayed this prayer out loud, the Bible says you have instantly become a new creature in Christ:

"old things have passed away, behold all things are new" (2 Corinthians 5:17). You will never be the same. Now you need to find a good local church and get involved as part of the family of God. Find a church that will love and care for you, and teach you the Word of God.

Destiny: Finding God's Plan and Purpose for Your Life
Pastor Michael Cameneti

In today's society, destiny is often defined as a place in life you'll eventually arrive at, regardless of the effort you put toward reaching it; but that way of thinking is far from the truth. God has authored a specific plan for your life; so specific that every detail is penned in a book in Heaven. It is His desire that you follow that plan and fulfill the destiny He has preordained for you.

5-tape audio series **$20⁰⁰** #1162

Home Improvement
Pastor Michael Cameneti

Statistics show that in the world today, 50% of marriages end in divorce. With this staggering figure, we need to examine the blueprint for building and maintaining a strong marriage and family. In this series, Pastor Michael Cameneti examines the basic building blocks needed for structuring a solid family and home.

8-tape audio series **$32⁰⁰** #1144

Winning the Battle of the Mind
Pastor Michael Cameneti

It has been said that all faith battles are either won or lost in the mind. You will learn how you can renew your mind, so that your spirit will dominate you in this life! There is a way to complete victory by putting off the old thoughts and putting on the new.

7-tape audio series **$28⁰⁰** #1149

Grace: God's Plan for Man
Pastor Michael Cameneti

The grace of God encompasses His ability, His unmerited favor, His loving kindness – and He provided it for you as a free gift; it's not something you can earn. As you go with Pastor Mike through the Word of God, you will be compelled to transform your thinking to "grace thinking" and begin to see yourself and others through the eyes of God.

5-tape audio series **$20⁰⁰** #1163

About
Canton Christian Fellowship™
A Church to Call Home™

Pastors Michael &
Barbara Cameneti

Pastors Mike and Barb Cameneti, under the direction of the Holy Spirit, established Canton Christian Fellowship in the winter of 1988. Today, CCF has grown into a large, diverse, and multi-faceted ministry, impacting people of all ages in our community and beyond. Sensitive to the leading of the Holy Spirit, Pastors Mike and Barb boldly minister the uncompromised Word of God clearly and accurately, with the gifts of the Spirit accompanying the preaching of the Word.

It is our desire to provide an environment where you and your family will experience the goodness of God and His abounding love toward you. If you do not have a home church and live in the Canton area, we invite you to be a part of our church family. At Canton Christian Fellowship, we're "A Church to Call Home."

Pastor Mike can also be seen on our *Keys to Victorious Living*™ television broadcast every week. Check our website for program listings.

Keys to
Victorious
Living™

Contact Information:
5305 Broadmoor Circle NW. Canton, Ohio 44709
www.ccfchurch.com • 330-492-0925